THE TRAFFICKER NEXT DOOR

ALSO BY RHACEL SALAZAR PARREÑAS

Unfree:
Migrant Domestic Work in Arab States

Servants of Globalization:
Migration and Domestic Work

Children of Global Migration:
Transnational Families and Gendered Woes

Illicit Flirtations:
Labor, Migration, and Sex Trafficking in Tokyo

The Force of Domesticity:
Filipina Migrants and Globalization

NORTON
SHORTS

THE TRAFFICKER NEXT DOOR

How Household Employers Exploit Domestic Workers

RHACEL SALAZAR PARREÑAS

W. W. NORTON & COMPANY
Independent Publishers Since 1923

Copyright © 2025 by Rhacel Salazar Parreñas

All rights reserved
Printed in the United States of America
First Edition

For information about permission to reproduce selections
from this book, write to Permissions, W. W. Norton & Company, Inc.,
500 Fifth Avenue, New York, NY 10110

For information about special discounts for bulk purchases,
please contact W. W. Norton Special Sales at
specialsales@wwnorton.com or 800-233-4830

Manufacturing by Lakeside Book Company
Production manager: Delaney Adams

ISBN: 978-1-324-02030-1

W. W. Norton & Company, Inc.
500 Fifth Avenue, New York, NY 10110
www.wwnorton.com

W. W. Norton & Company Ltd.
15 Carlisle Street, London W1D 3BS

10 9 8 7 6 5 4 3 2 1

CONTENTS

AUTHOR'S NOTE	ix
INTRODUCTION: The Trafficker Next Door	1
CHAPTER 1: A Modern-Day American Slave	21
CHAPTER 2: The Risks Migrants Take	51
CHAPTER 3: Exploiters of Forced Labor	77
CONCLUSION: How to Fight Forced Labor	110
ACKNOWLEDGMENTS	123
GLOSSARY	125
NOTES	127
INDEX	143

AUTHOR'S NOTE

This book draws on 20 years of my sociological research on migrant domestic workers from the Philippines. I conducted participant observation in the United Arab Emirates, Singapore, and the Philippines and interviewed domestic workers in Los Angeles, Rome, Copenhagen, Dubai, and Singapore as well as employers in Los Angeles, Dubai, and Singapore. This book uses extensive field notes and interviews. I received approval for my research from the institutional review boards at the University of California, Berkeley, and the University of Southern California. Except for the writer Alex Tizon and his family's slave, Eudocia Pulido, I used pseudonyms. Tizon wrote about Pulido in *The Atlantic*, making his family's story public knowledge. In addition to using pseudonyms, I limited descriptive details. In some cases, I made slight changes to descriptive details such as a person's occupation. I did not alter demographic characteristics such as gender and nationality. I used anonymized first names for employers and domestic workers when they themselves insisted on being referred to by their first name during the interview.

THE TRAFFICKER NEXT DOOR

INTRODUCTION

THE TRAFFICKER NEXT DOOR

Sir Mohamed Farah's story is remarkable. He overcame extreme childhood poverty to become the greatest British long-distance runner in history. He won gold medals in the 5,000-meter and 10,000-meter races at both the 2012 and 2016 Olympic Games. In 2017, Queen Elizabeth II knighted Farah in recognition of his extraordinary contributions to British sports.

But Farah had a secret: As a child, he was trafficked to the United Kingdom from Djibouti and subjected to domestic servitude. He shared his story publicly in the 2022 documentary *The Real Mo Farah*. We learn in the documentary that his birth name is Hussein Abdi Kahin. He was born in Somalia. His father, Abdi, was killed by stray shrapnel from a bazooka explosion while working in the fields during the Somali civil war when Farah was just four years old. Unable to care for him and his twin brother on her own, their mother sent them to live with a relative in Djibouti. The brothers lived in squalor in a makeshift house with dirt floors and rusty corrugated-metal siding in a crowded neighborhood with unpaved streets. It was there that a nine-year-old Farah met a woman who offered to rescue him and his brother from poverty. She was joining her husband in the United Kingdom and invited the siblings to accompany her under the guise that she would help connect them with family in Europe.

As it happened, she took only Farah, who she pretended was her son. Traveling with forged documents, Farah entered the United Kingdom under the assumed name of Mohamed Muktar Jama Farah. Not long after landing in the United Kingdom, Farah realized that the woman had no intention of helping him reunite with his relatives in Holland. He recalled, "I had all the contact details for my relatives and once we got to her house, the lady . . . ripped them up and put it in the bin and at that moment I knew I was in trouble."

Farah was treated more like a slave than kin. "I wasn't treated as part of the family," he shared in the documentary. He continued: "I was always that kid who did everything . . . someone, like, who works for you. . . . If I wanted food in my mouth, my job was to look after those kids. [I] showered them, cook for them, cleaned for them. And she said, if you ever want to see your family again, don't say anything. If you say anything, they will take you away."

Farah did not regularly attend school in the United Kingdom until he was 11 years old. He got into fights, was disruptive in class, and struggled to keep up with schoolwork. Running was his only escape, and he was good at it. He was even selected to represent Great Britain in an international running competition in Latvia but was unable to participate because of his lack of travel documents.

When he was 14 years old, Farah confided in his PE coach, Alan Watkinson, who contacted social services. Watkinson helped find Farah another home, and then worked on securing his British nationality.

Farah's experience did not fit early definitions of human trafficking. In 1991, the year Farah was trafficked to the United Kingdom, the concept of "trafficking" was associated only with prostitution, defined as the "procuring of women or girls for immoral purposes abroad" in the 1904 International Agreement for the Suppression of the "White Slave Traffic." Only in 2000 did the United Nations expand its definition of trafficking to more broadly refer to the transportation of someone under false pretenses for the purpose of their exploitation.

Why was Farah trafficked? What were the circumstances that led to his trafficking? The woman who trafficked Farah opted not to participate in the documentary, which was aired on BBC. She did eventually share her side of the story. Speaking to the British tabloid newspaper *The Sun* through her 33-year-old son, Ahmed, she claimed she did nothing wrong. Even Ahmed vehemently denied Farah's accusations: "I have a very clear memory of my childhood. We would all be told, 'Go clean your room,' and given chores like in any other house—everyone had to pull their weight. Mum treated Mo like her own son and we would play together all the time." According to Ahmed, his mother saved Farah from a life of poverty. By taking him to the United Kingdom, which has a universal health-care system, she supposedly helped Farah get treatment for severe burns he suffered on his arm as a child. We do not know if this is true, as it is a subject not publicly acknowledged by Farah. It is, however, unlikely, as there are no visible burn scars on Farah that would support this claim. Ahmed shares, "My mum said that she risked everything for him to come with us and treated him like her own son just to be accused of these terrible things."

How do we resolve the narrative disagreement between trafficked and trafficker? I do not doubt that Farah was trafficked. His experience mirrors that of countless children, including *filhas de criação*, or "raised daughters," in Brazil; *restavek* in Haiti; and child domestic workers in Ghana. All perform menial household tasks for little to no pay. Yet I also think that Ahmed's mother genuinely believes she did nothing wrong. She likely saw herself as Farah's savior, freeing him from a life of destitution in Africa. For this, she likely thought that having him do housework, even as a child, was fair compensation. This logic, which I call the *employer savior complex*, is common among domestic employers and, as I will show in this book, is one that keeps alive a system of domestic subjugation that remains prevalent today.

THIS IS A BOOK on human trafficking, specifically the abuse of domestic workers in the intimate space of the home. Popular media depicts human trafficking as an extraordinary crime fueled by underground crime syndicates that kidnap, enslave, and exploit innocent victims for profit. An iconic example would be the movie *Taken*, in which an ex–CIA operative, played by Liam Neeson, is given 96 hours to rescue his teenage daughter from an Albanian sex-trafficking ring that abducts and sells innocent American tourists in Paris to wealthy Arab men. This story is reminiscent of a forced-prostitution case in the 1990s. The Cadena brothers lured Mexican women from their hometown of Veracruz and trafficked them to Florida with false promises of legitimate employment in the United States. However, it's important to point out that these women, unlike the character in *Taken*, were not kidnapped. They willingly went with the men in the hopes of creating a better life for themselves. This is typical: Victims of trafficking take risks out of financial desperation only to be abused by the people they trusted to help them.

Modern-day slavery, including human trafficking, has grown in the past few decades. In part, this growth is the result of a broadened definition of slavery. Historically, slavery was understood solely as a system of property ownership. Many individuals still abide by the 1926 Slavery Convention, which presents a narrow definition as chattel slavery, meaning legal ownership of another human being. The classic example of this type of enslavement is the experience of millions of African men, women, and children during the transatlantic slave trade. But at its heart, slavery is a relationship of economic exploitation. Modern-day slavery includes any form of encroachment on the freedom of individuals, including trafficking, debt bondage, and indenture. Kevin Bales, founder of Free the Slaves, defines enslavement as the control of a person by another person for the purpose of their economic exploitation. Under this looser conception, slavery extends beyond chattel slavery to include peonage, meaning debt bondage or a situation in which a person uses their labor to pay off a significant debt; "contract slavery," which refers to the situation of migrant workers who are contractually bound to work for another person without flexibility to quit their job; and finally, forced labor, meaning work performed involuntarily or under the threat of penalty.

A challenge facing researchers and activists is a lack of verifiable statistics. Reports often claim there are 27 million victims of modern-day slavery. That statistic has appeared in CNN reports, the annual U.S. State Department *Trafficking in Persons Report*, and a speech by former U.S. Secretary of State Antony Blinken. But the 27-million figure is nothing more than an estimate provided nearly

20 years ago by Bales, who admits that it was just a "good guess" based on a "great hodge podge" of data.

Since 2013, Bales himself has turned to the Global Slavery Index, which measures the prevalence of slavery across the globe and is considered the most comprehensive dataset on modern-day slavery. The Global Slavery Index increased its estimate of the global enslaved population to 29.8 million in 2013 and then to 50 million in 2023. The index is administered by Walk Free, an international organization funded by Australian billionaire Andrew Forrest, who has embraced the eradication of slavery as a personal mission. But Anne Gallagher, a former adviser on trafficking to the UN High Commissioner for Human Rights, argues that the index's methods are unreliable because it extrapolates from sample data from just 19 countries to account for enslavement in 167 countries. Both figures, 27 million and 50 million, circulate as zombie statistics, figures that despite their questionable origins become common knowledge due to repeated citation.

Numbers that are perhaps more reliable come from the International Labour Organization (ILO), which published a report in 2017 suggesting that there are 24.9 million individuals trapped in forced labor. They include 16 million persons exploited in the private sector, such as domestic, construction, or agricultural employment; 4.8 million persons in forced sexual exploitation; and 4.1 million persons in state-imposed forced labor, such as work carried out by prisoners and detainees or compulsory labor by citizens during harvest season. But even these figures are mere estimates extrapolated from a survey of 71,000 individuals across 48 countries.

The unreliability of these numbers does not deny the problem of trafficking. Our fixation with numbers, however, misguides us, as numbers do not explain how and why trafficking occurs. Unreliable data do point to something we know, which is that labor trafficking, not sex trafficking, is a more pervasive form of human trafficking. False narratives of sex trafficking only distort our understanding of the problem.

The more lurid forms of exploitation, organ removal and sexual abuse, and the fears that animate the movie *Taken*—the abuse of innocent young women, abductions by malicious, foreign actors, international crime syndicates disrupting law and order—resonate widely. Here again, we don't have reliable data: According to one zombie statistic, 80 percent of trafficking victims are female, with 70 percent trafficked in the commercial sex industry. These figures are dangerous because they both prevent us from fully understanding the problem and redirect us from designing evidence-based solutions. According to criminologist Sheldon Zhang, this unproven claim has led to the funneling of government attention and resources into the investigation and prosecution of johns. This myth also directs research. Sociologist Katharine Donato and historian Donna Gabaccia found that sex trafficking accounts for one-third of all scholarly publications on women's migration since 1983. Yet much of this work, according to them, is not based on empirically grounded research.

Besides the basic fact that sex sells in popular media, stories of sex trafficking touch on deeper cultural narratives. For example, anthropologist Carole Vance suggests that our obsession with sex trafficking is fueled by the melodrama of white male heroism. This means that anti-trafficking is not just a story of women's subjugation but also one of men rescuing women. We see this in films such as *Sound of Freedom*, a 2023 crime thriller based on the real-life experience of the anti-trafficking crusader Tim Ballard and the writings of men such as Bales. These men have publicly declared the rescue of trafficked victims, particularly women, as their life mission. British scholars Jo Doezema and Laura Lammasniemi separately argue that the narrative of heroism is a legacy of 19th-century white-slavery abolition campaigns, in which heroic white men were called to save innocent white women from foreign men. Modern-day calls for "heroes" by news groups such as CNN and the U.S. government in its *Trafficking in Persons Report* reinforce such narratives.

This is not to say that sex trafficking does not exist. It does. Victims of the Cadena brothers can attest to this. Yet inflated figures on sex trafficking prevent us from understanding the problem, in part because they elicit a "moral panic," panic around an exaggerated threat against societal values that is often fueled and maintained by media coverage. Zombie statistics and moral panic leave us in a poor position to design solutions to modern-day slavery.

Further clouding the picture is the supposed inaccessibility of victims. According to the UN Office on Drugs and Crime, there is little empirical evidence on trafficking "because the crime takes place underground and is often not identified or misidentified." Sociologist Ronald Weitzer disagrees. He maintains that the lack of data is the result of a misguided focus on quantifying the problem to establish its validity. To understand the problem of human trafficking and accordingly develop solutions for it, Weitzer argues, we need to put aside our obsession with numbers and focus instead on documenting the everyday experiences of victims in their social settings. As he points out, we can study targeted populations, including hard-to-reach victims of sex trafficking, by using qualitative research methods such as interviews and participant observation.

Weitzer supported his conclusions with data from an ethnographic study I conducted in 2005. The subject of the study was Filipino entertainers in the nightlife industry of Tokyo. These workers had been identified by the U.S. Department of State as victims of forced prostitution in its annual *Trafficking in Persons Report*. I later learned this to be a false assertion after working side by side with them. It is true that some entertainers provided sex. Yet if they did, it was likely by choice. We would not think this based on the U.S. government report, which describes these women as being "stripped of their passports and travel documents and forced into situations of sexual exploitation." The *Trafficking in Persons Report*, which has been repeatedly criticized by scholars for its use of unreliable methods, provided no more than a speculation, but a powerful one that has turned into a zombie fact, something believed to be true even after being disproved.

The United States officially began to monitor the problem of human trafficking in 2000 when Congress passed the Victims of Trafficking and Violence Protection Act, declaring itself the "global sheriff" tasked with eliminating this problem. Through the newly formed Office to Monitor and Combat Trafficking in Persons, in 2001 the United States began to publish an annual report with a country-by-country assessment of efforts to eliminate the problem. Notably, while the U.S. government initially tasked itself with monitoring trafficking across the globe, it didn't include itself in its annual report until 2010. In initial publications of the *Trafficking in Persons Report*, the United States claimed that there were 700,000 victims of human trafficking globally, most of whom were women and children. This is in sharp contrast to the 27 million estimated count provided by Bales around the same time. The more conservative estimate in the *Trafficking in Persons Report* is not necessarily the product of more accurate methodology. In fact, the U.S. Government Accountability Office has repeatedly criticized this report for its use of shoddy methods.

Yet if there had indeed been 700,000 victims of trafficking as claimed in the *Trafficking in Persons Report*, then the women I worked alongside in Japan, identified as victims of sexual exploitation, would have constituted more than 10 percent of them. According to official reports from the Philippines, 80,000 Filipina entertainers were employed in Japan at the time I was conducting research. I worked with them in a bar owned by a member of an organized crime syndicate, or *yakuza*, and found that while forced prostitution could occur, it was rare. The job of Filipina entertainers in Japan is to flirt with customers. They engage customers in conversation and even sing and dance for them. The most skilled can string a customer along for months, luring them back to the club with the promise of sex that both she and the customer know is unlikely to occur. The provision of sex squashes the titillation that repeatedly draws customers to the club, which is why sex is ultimately discouraged by management. To engage in prostitution is bad for the business of entertainers.

While forced prostitution was unlikely, my co-workers were susceptible to other forms of forced labor due to the conditions of their employment. Not only were they restricted to work in the one bar that sponsored their visa, they also had their wages withheld until the end of their six-month contract. The common practice in Japan was to pay them at the airport before they boarded their flight back to the Philippines. This meant that they were unable to quit their jobs without forfeiting their wages. As a result, they often had to deal with unwanted advances, including, in my case, a regular customer who liked to practice his shiatsu techniques on my pressure points.

My research in Japan showed me that human trafficking is not just a matter of villainous traffickers, vulnerable women, and heroic saviors, but a problem caused by restrictive conditions of labor and migration. Medical anthropologists such as Philippe Bourgois call this "structural vulnerability," a situation where conditions put individuals at risk of negative outcomes. This goes against popular discourse. The narratives of widespread sex trafficking and the heroic labors of male crusaders erroneously suggest that modern-day slavery is an individual as opposed to a structural problem. Anthropologist Denise Brennan's work also counters the heroism narrative that dominates trafficking discourse. Her research, which follows the lives of human-trafficking survivors in the United States, points to exclusionary immigration laws as a key structural cause of modern-day slavery. Draconian migration policies deny legal pathways for workers in low-wage jobs and thereby create undocumented workers who are then denied labor protection or given little recourse against abusive employers. These workers, according to Brennan, are more likely to tolerate subpar labor conditions.

Yet, while harsh migration policies and structural conditions often enable exploitation, trafficking or slavery ultimately happens because individuals take advantage of their power and act on the structural vulnerability of others. In the case of entertainers in Japan, the bar owners can act on their power by refusing to let entertainers quit. They can exploit the authority they wield over their employees due to structural conditions such as exclusionary immigration laws, poor labor regulation, debt bondage, and indenture. Similarly,

Farah's host enforced her power over him, isolating him and then threatening him with deportation if he told the truth.

The conditions of migrant entertainers in Japan are notably like those of other groups of migrant workers vulnerable to trafficking, especially domestic workers. Identifying them as victims of sex trafficking rather than labor trafficking hid this similarity. Rather than perpetuate narratives that focus only on sexual exploitation, this book focuses on the ways in which domestic workers, including young ones like Farah, are being exploited, trafficked, and enslaved. Not only is this situation more common than sexual slavery, but it also touches many more lives and implicates many more people—including employers who otherwise consider themselves good people yet may unwittingly become traffickers themselves.

THERE ARE 67 MILLION domestic workers globally, a figure drawn by the ILO from national data sources. They represent a group acutely vulnerable to trafficking, with the most at risk being the estimated 11.5 million migrant workers. According to a 2022 report by the ILO, domestic workers—the vast majority of whom are women—constitute 8.2 percent of the supposed 17.3 million victims of forced-labor exploitation. This is a drop from the estimated 24 percent of 24.9 million victims given in 2017. The ILO, which claims to have used similar methodology in the two reports, doesn't explain this dramatic change.

Discussions of modern-day slavery and forced labor sit shoulder to shoulder with the problem of human trafficking. Trafficking, as defined by the United Nations, refers to a three-part process in which someone is (1) transported (2) under dubious or coerced conditions (3) for the purpose of their exploitation. The range of potential exploitations is wide and includes servitude, slavery, and slavery-like practices such as debt bondage, forced labor, sexual exploitation, and the removal of organs.

While we cannot fully (or solely) rely on numbers to tell us how many trafficked victims there actually are today, structural conditions can confirm the vulnerability of particular groups to labor trafficking. This would be the case for migrant domestic workers. Their standard employment conditions, as this book illustrates, include legal indenture, debt bondage, and the absence of labor protection. These conditions are not exceptional to a particular region or country. Instead, they are pervasive and apply to migrant domestic workers in many countries, including England, Israel, Malaysia, Turkey, Singapore, United Arab Emirates, and the United States.

Many domestic-labor arrangements described in this book will seem shocking to American readers, who imagine that similar exploitation would never take place in the United States or other Western countries. But it does. Take the case of au pairs in the United States. Every year approximately 13,000 au pairs enter the United States under the J-1 Exchange Visitor Program. Implemented as early as 1961 to facilitate scientific and cultural exchanges between the United States and select foreign countries, the J-1 program allows students, teachers, and other scholars to receive training for a temporary period in the United States. It did not include au pairs until 1986. That year, a private company, the U.S. Information Agency, now known as the American Institute of Foreign Study, established a pilot program to bring 3,000 young Western Europeans as au pairs into the country for a two-year period. This program has since expanded globally, with the largest group of participants coming from Germany, Brazil, France, Colombia, and Mexico.

Like domestic workers in other countries, au pairs lack recognition as workers. In the United States, au pairs are considered "exchange visitors." As such, their temporary migration is administered by the U.S. Department of State, not the Department of Labor. Because of this arrangement, host families are spared stringent background checks, including scrutiny of their employment history. In effect, host families with documented cases of au pair abuse can continue to sponsor them. Such was the case for Intel manager Ashish Gupta of Oregon. On October 5, 2011, a German au pair filed a lawsuit accusing U.S. Au Pair Inc. of fraud and negligence for placing her in Gupta's home. The lawsuit claimed that the agency had failed to disclose reported cases of sexual abuse from two of Gupta's previous au pairs. The agency denied the accusation.

Most au pairs can be found in California, Washington, DC, New York, and Illinois, where they are exempt from state labor laws and earn significantly less than the state minimum wage. For example, despite the fact that the minimum wage is more than $16 an hour in California and New York, au pairs receive an artificially low wage rate of $4.35 an hour. While they are legally entitled to the federal minimum wage of $7.25 per hour, they receive much less because host families can deduct up to 40 percent of the au pair's wages for room-and-board expenses. In contrast, most other countries, including the Kingdom of Saudi Arabia, do not allow employers to charge domestic workers for their accommodations.

Adding to au pairs' vulnerability is their precarious legal status. Like domestic workers in other countries, au pairs' legal residency is contingent on their continuous employment as a live-in worker in one household. Indenture engenders abuse because it encourages workers to tolerate subpar labor conditions; demanding better work conditions could result in deportation. As indentured workers, au pairs are given only a two-week window to secure a new sponsor if they are fired or quit their job. Deportation is a risk many cannot afford, as they have often incurred debts ranging from $500 to $2,500—an exorbitant sum for many migrants—to cover the fees imposed by the au pair agency.

The au pair program mirrors the migrant labor regimes for domestic workers in other countries. These regimes are set up to create indentured workers who are beholden to a sponsor with the power to fire and deport them at will. Having this power should raise a moral dilemma for American families who choose to sponsor au pairs as well as for those who sponsor the migration of domestic workers elsewhere. These employers can easily become unwitting traffickers.

I have been studying domestic workers for more than two decades. My research among au pairs in Copenhagen and domestic workers in Dubai, Los Angeles, and Singapore shows that employers manage their authority in different ways. Some provide positive labor conditions, including high wages, adequate accommodations, and plenty of free time. But others take advantage of their authority. As documented by organizations such as the National Domestic Workers Alliance and Polaris Project, there are Americans who deny au pairs a day off, commit wage theft, feed them inadequately, do not provide acceptable accommodations, and sexually harass them. The abuse of au pairs raises many questions: How do employers justify denying domestic workers basic human rights? What contexts cause them to mistreat workers to the point of slavery? How do they become "the trafficker next door"?

CURIOUSLY, EMPLOYERS ARE OFTEN unconscious of their own bad behavior. When they limit domestic workers to one meal a day, they manage to see the provision of that one meal as generosity. After all, they reason, this domestic worker had little to eat before they migrated; now they have more (even if it's not enough). Similarly, employers who insist that their live-in domestic workers sleep in the kitchen reframe this as generously providing the worker safer, more secure, and better lodging than they enjoyed in their home country.

I call this moral justification the "employer savior complex." By this logic, employers portray their actions as having socially worthy or moral purposes. The employer savior complex argues that the worker would have a much worse life if not employed in their household, and that one's employment of a domestic worker provides the worker a pathway away from poverty and suffering.

At its core, the employer savior complex decouples exploitation and mistreatment. It is a concept that borrows from what Teju Cole calls the "white-savior industrial complex," which describes the pattern of white people rescuing and freeing people of color from their suffering for the purpose of self-validation. Employers similarly feel good about themselves when they rescue someone from supposed poverty and hire them as a domestic worker. In my fieldwork I encountered dozens of employers who expressed some version of the employer savior complex. Carolyn, a wealthy British expat in Dubai, admitted that she emotionally and verbally abused her household staff. Carolyn insisted that it was nearly impossible to exploit domestic workers in Dubai because, as she argued, whatever their living and working conditions may be, their life could only be better than whatever it had been prior to migration. Carolyn paid her domestic workers less than an average salary yet insisted that the low wages offered mobility for an otherwise impoverished worker from a poor country like the Philippines, where prior to migration they "lived in rags" but now are "very, very wealthy in their [friends'] eyes." To an employer like Carolyn, leftovers are better than starvation, sleeping in the hallway is better than houselessness, and a minuscule salary is better than none. As Carolyn explained, "Anyone who thinks that the maids here are exploited and underpaid doesn't realize how much the money they are paid is worth to them in their home countries."

Many domestic employers, including in the United States, would agree, including my own mother. I recall coming home from college once to find a young Mexican couple, a domestic worker employed by my family, and her husband, living in my parents' garage. My parents lived in a semiarid region far east of Los Angeles where temperatures boiled in the summers. When I questioned these abysmal living conditions, my mother responded, "This is much better than their situation in Mexico."

Then there is the case of Harit "Potee" Saluja. Saluja was accused in 2011 of trafficking by two other Indians, who claimed they worked for Saluja for 13 hours each day for less than minimum wage. In response to this accusation, Saluja shared with a news reporter, "You know, sometimes people do come to live with you. It's not like you don't be kind. This is the result of kindness." Saluja likely saw their accommodations in the basement of her Long Island home and compensation of less than $300 per month as an improvement over their life in India.

The employer savior complex is not new. People throughout history have found ways to justify immoral acts that infringe on the human rights of others. In 19th-century America, Vice President John C. Calhoun saw slavery as a benevolent institution that brought "positive good" and civilized those from a "low, degraded and savage condition." Former congressman James Henry Hammond saw slavery as providing humane conditions to those who otherwise could not care for themselves. In the same way that slave owners used the logic of moral justification to defend slavery in the 1800s, employers today do the same to deflect from their own poor treatment of domestic workers.

In my fieldwork in the United Arab Emirates, the United States, and Singapore, I have seen how certain cultural practices enable unique expressions of the employer savior complex. In the United Arab Emirates, Orientalism—the view of Arab society as backward and barbaric—allows Western employers to downplay the mistreatment of domestic workers with the racist belief that their bad behavior cannot be worse than those of their Arab neighbors. In the United States, we see migrant communities use the cultural practice of bartering and trading children for domestic labor to justify wage theft. In countries such as Brazil, Ghana, Haiti, and the Philippines, families will sometimes "adopt" children of poorer relatives in exchange for their labor, paying them in "education" instead of in cash. This cultural system shapes the understanding of domestic work in some migrant households in the United States. A major case study in this book will be Alex Tizon, a Filipino American author and Pulitzer Prize–winning journalist who justified his family's enslavement of an unpaid domestic worker for more than 50 years by explaining how she came to work for his family through such a cultural pathway, and suggesting that their treatment of her was justified because they had rescued her from poverty.

My research has revealed other modes of deflection as well. Employers often selectively infantilize workers, assuming they are rational adults when they choose to become migrant laborers but then imagining them to be childlike in managing other aspects of their freedom. Employers are also influenced by social norms that help them justify pushing aside personal morality and participating in exploitative systems. Take, for instance, an American who relocates to Singapore in order to earn higher wages and also to take advantage of the country's lack of a minimum wage when hiring a domestic worker. After hiring the worker for a "bargain" not possible in the United States, they then subject the worker to debt bondage by withholding their worker's wages for up to the first eight months of employment to cover the hiring agency fees. They justify this by explaining that it's standard practice in the economic culture of migrant labor. In other words, there is a market that creates jobs for otherwise destitute migrant domestic workers and market participation has its costs, which in this case includes paltry wages and debt bondage. Employers also shield themselves in a cloak of what theorists describe as "pernicious ignorance," which broadly allows the employer to avoid looking too carefully at the situation from the worker's perspective and prevents them from questioning prevailing labor standards or systems (such as labor agencies) that impose heavy costs on workers. Beyond these structures, there are other aspects at play in certain domestic environments, including the ideology of female domesticity, which refers to the notion that women are supposed to inhabit the private sphere and care for their family with little to no remuneration.

This book will explore all these justifications and more. In doing so, I hope to shed light on the situation of many other vulnerable groups, including those fleeing wars in Eastern Europe and the Middle East and destitution in Asia and South America. Venezuelans who pay high fees to flee the country may find themselves in harm's way. Inevitably, an opportunistic capitalist will take advantage of them by offering them jobs they cannot leave, such as in coca plantations in Colombia. Burmese fishermen may willingly participate in their illegal smuggling and cross the jungle into Thailand by foot only to be trapped and abused in Thai vessels. Syrians fleeing to Germany may pay smugglers and risk abandonment at the border of Hungary. Desperation fuels vulnerability. And unfortunately, many people will take advantage of that vulnerability. The specific contexts in which this occurs are what I aim to explain in this book. By observing the lives of workers and employers in several settings around the world, I hope to illuminate some of the structural and personal reasons people accept the risks of becoming migrant laborers, and how employers—even well-meaning ones—can unwittingly become the trafficker next door.

CHAPTER 1

A MODERN-DAY AMERICAN SLAVE

SLAVERY EXISTS IN the United States today but not many people recognize it, partly because modern-day slavery looks different from the system of chattel slavery that existed prior to the American Civil War. But a 2017 *Atlantic* cover article by Pulitzer Prize–winning journalist Alex Tizon exploded the myth of its nonexistence. Published posthumously, Tizon's essay revealed that his family had owned a slave for 56 years. "I had a family, a career, a house in the suburbs—the American dream. And then I had a slave," admits Tizon. Her name was Eudocia Tomas Pulido, but she was known as Lola Cosiang to her family. Her enslavement began in 1943 when a 12-year-old Leticia Asuncion, Tizon's mother, received the 18-year-old Pulido as a gift from her father, Tomas Asuncion. Pulido's enslavement continued when Leticia married, had a family, and relocated from the Philippines to the United States. Her enslavement ended, according to Tizon, when Leticia passed away in 1999. At this point, Pulido moved in with Tizon and finally began to receive financial compensation for her labor, albeit only $200 per week.

Tizon insinuates that his mother's subjugation of Pulido was both a curse and a blessing. Her bondage led to a life of misery. Her labor conditions were abysmal: "Wasn't paid. Toiled every day. Was tongue-lashed for sitting too long or falling asleep too early. Was struck for talking back. Wore hand-me-downs. Ate scraps and leftovers by herself in the kitchen. Rarely left the house. Had no friends or hobbies outside the family. Had no private quarters." She was also denied an intimate life and likely died a virgin at 86 years old. Yet, according to Tizon, her subjugation was also a blessing, in that it offered a pathway out of an undesirable marriage to an older man and a life of abject poverty in the Philippines. While Tizon admits his family mistreated Pulido, he also suggests things could have been worse. Two of her younger siblings got sick and died early in life.

Tizon's essay is written in an emotionally affecting way, and his storytelling subtly deflects blame from himself and his mother. He explains how his mother says she never wanted a servant, and how Tizon's father, whom Tizon portrays unsympathetically in the story, was the one who convinced Pulido to come to the United States with false promises of an allowance. He positions himself as being innocent in her enslavement, uncomfortable with her treatment, and ultimately an ally for her in that he pushes his mother to treat Pulido better. He suggests that he stopped this campaign only when Pulido herself asked him to. Further, he candidly describes his mother's verbal cruelty toward Pulido but also relates how the two women shared intimate moments, including a scene where Leticia cries in Pulido's lap, another where Pulido defends Leticia from her second husband during a domestic dispute, and finally a poignant deathbed scene: "The priest asked Mom whether there was anything she wanted to forgive or be forgiven for. She scanned the room with heavy-lidded eyes, said nothing. Then, without looking at Lola, she reached over and placed an open hand on her head."

Tizon then describes how Pulido flourished under his care, learning to read (albeit on her own, without help from Tizon), tending her garden, and enjoying other semiretired activities. He explains that he tried to convince her not to work. And even though she continued to cook and clean and helped raise his children he took pride in seeing her once with her feet up and a puzzle in her hand. He writes, "*Progress*, I thought." He also makes a point to explain that he paid for her to travel to the Philippines so she might see if she wanted to live there. He says that in the end she herself decided to return "home" to live with Tizon in the United States. Upon witnessing her death from a heart attack, Tizon writes, "She'd had none of the self-serving ambition that drives most of us, and her willingness to give up everything for the people around her won her our love and utter loyalty. She's become a hallowed figure in my extended family." The story ends with Tizon returning Pulido's ashes to her grateful relatives, who are finally able to grieve.

Tizon is explicit that Pulido was a slave. Yet he suggests that she ceased being a slave when his mother died and Pulido came to live with Tizon's family. Pulido's late-life experience still bears many hallmarks of modern-day slavery. Harvard sociologist Orlando Patterson challenges us to see slavery as a particular experience of suffering, a state of being that includes subjection to violence; erasure of dignity; natal alienation, or forced separation from birth kin; and lastly, denial of manumission, that is, freedom or release from slavery. Pulido experienced these things and more—she was denied pay, denied education, denied a romantic life, and separated from her family and home. Pulido's story illuminates how people who otherwise consider themselves upstanding citizens may become traffickers. Ultimately, one of the Tizon family's most pernicious acts was viewing Pulido as a family member, someone whom they claimed to love and who they felt loved them in return.

Pulido's story sparked intense debate. Many readers were appalled to learn a woman had been held as a slave more than a century after the Civil War. Yet others questioned whether she had really been a slave. The circumstances of Pulido's transfer to Leticia from Leticia's father are unclear. Likewise hazy is why Pulido's family would send her to fill such a lowly position in someone else's household. Or why Pulido herself would agree to this arrangement. Then there remain the questions of why Pulido tolerated her situation for so long or why, upon Leticia's death, Pulido chose to stay with Tizon even after he gave her the option to return to the Philippines. Pointing to Pulido's complacency and resignation, some commentators questioned the severity of her suffering. If she had really been a slave, they reasoned, she would have had a greater will to liberate herself.

Others went further and argued that calling Pulido a slave was a misreading and, worse, an attack on Philippine culture. Many of these critics were experts on Southeast Asia by either scholarship or experience. They argued for a narrow, chattel-based definition of slavery. Because "Pulido was not property who could be bought and sold," writes the Southeast Asian historian Vicente Rafael for *The Atlantic*, she had not been subject to "slavery" as we understand it in the United States. Rafael further contends that we must see Pulido's subjugation as part of a "complex relationship," and suggests that those outraged by Pulido's condition fail to engage Philippine culture. Rafael dismisses the critics of Tizon's family as at best ignorant and at worst ethnocentric.

Espousing a cultural defense, Rafael suggests that domestic servitude in the Philippines cannot be compared to chattel slavery because it does not embody property ownership but instead is premised on a kind of debt bondage, which is not a permanent state. While there has been a system of slavery in the Philippines, one that ties individuals to a master, its economic arrangement is different from how we understand it to be in the United States. There are two types of "slaves" in the Philippines, Rafael explains: *alipin sagigilid* (or "slave in the corners"), referring to those who live in the master's house and are on call 24/7, and *alipin namamahay* (or "slave who is housed"), meaning those who have their own dwelling and seasonally provide labor to the master. In either case, an *alipin*, which means "slave," can eventually secure their freedom and pay off their debt through labor for or marriage with a free person According to Rafael, Pulido fits the category of *alipin sagigilid*. "Slaves" like Pulido are usually "poor relatives who had fallen on hard times." Indeed, Tizon described her as "a cousin from a marginal side of the family, rice farmers . . . penniless, unschooled, and likely to be malleable." For Rafael, because Pulido and others like her in the Philippines can eventually secure their freedom, they cannot be considered "slaves" in the context of the United States, where manumission was nearly impossible prior to slavery's abolition in 1865.

Yet Pulido's situation does not quite fit the definition of slavery in the Philippines for the simple reason that Pulido had not been in debt. She came to care for Leticia in exchange for "food and shelter." This discrepancy makes her situation culturally inexplicable, considering slavery's definition as a repayment of debt. In some ways, her circumstance is more akin to the practice of bartering children, such as the *restavek* in Haiti or *filhas de criação* in Brazil, who do housework in the homes of wealthier (often distant) relatives in exchange for food, shelter, and education. Rafael speculates that Pulido did incur debt: "Entering into domestic service was Pulido's way of escaping forced marriage to an older man. She thereby incurred a kind of debt whose costs were steep."

To me, Rafael's stance is intellectual sophistry. By hierarchizing different types of slavery, Rafael dismisses the suffering that Pulido endured for more than 50 years. Adamant about a hierarchical differentiation between slavery in the United States and that in the Philippines, Rafael insinuates the latter to be less severe because it is not completely extractive and involves some form of reciprocity. Enslavers supposedly rescue slaves from debt or poor living conditions, and slaves in turn repay enslavers with labor. According to Rafael, this reciprocal exchange occurs in an affective and familial context, which in turn lends power to those in debt. Slaves in the Philippines, according to Rafael, are "a part of the family, albeit a lowly and exploited member." Rafael speculates that because they are members of the family, slaves can utilize affective ties to improve their situation, including *awa* (pity), *utang na loob* (reciprocal indebtedness) and *hiya* (shame).

Taking Tizon at his word, Rafael believes that Tizon's familial affection for Pulido eventually earned her a good life. For the last 12 years of her life, Pulido supposedly did not do much but, as Tizon put it, "sleep in, watch soaps, do nothing all day" and "relax—and be free—for the first time in her life." She also began to receive remuneration for her labor. For Rafael, this $200 per week marked the end of Pulido's enslavement and shifted the power dynamic between her and Tizon. As he explains, "In Filipino culture, these affective ties in turn provide servants—no matter how oppressive their situation—a kind of moral leverage that they can use to hold the master accountable."

Contrary to Rafael's argument, household workers cannot assume that membership in a family will improve labor conditions. We will discuss this in more detail later in the chapter, but for now we must recognize that the enslaver can also use the *idea* of the family to devalue the work of servants. This is an argument often advanced by experts on domestic work, who point out that familial bonds indicate vulnerability. As the research of Mary Romero shows, employers can manipulate these bonds to coerce domestic workers to tolerate subpar labor conditions. The enslaver's logic holds that it would be wrong for servants or slaves to expect compensation because "family" labors for love and not money. Following this logic, Pulido worked every day for five decades without compensation because she was a member of the family.

Tizon (and Rafael) would like us to believe that Pulido's enslavement ended when she moved in with Tizon's family. Tizon claims that he expected little of Pulido upon the death of his mother. He offered to let her move back to the Philippines and began paying her $200 each week. In his eyes, this was her moment of manumission, but as an expert on domestic work I would disagree. Manumission is rare in modern slave societies, as evidenced by a sweeping study of slavery in 66 societies by Patterson. According to Patterson, manumission was as low as 0.04 percent in the U.S. South, 0.17 percent in South Africa, 0.1 percent in Jamaica, and 3.2 percent in Colombia. Even in societies with a high rate of manumission, such as 18th- to early 19th-century Curaçao and Muslim Spain in AD 711–1492, rarely did it sever the unequal dependency between "ex-slave and ex-master." In other words, severe relations of economic inequality were often maintained upon manumission, with ex-masters still managing to extract labor for nearly nothing from ex-slaves. We can argue this was the case for Pulido, whose nominal salary prevented her from living a life truly independent of Tizon's family. I would argue that Pulido remained a slave after she chose to live with Tizon.

Yes, Pulido's economic condition shifted, and Tizon would like us to see his provision of a $200 weekly wage and free housing as both reparation for his mother's exploitation of Pulido and ongoing compensation for her time and labor. Putting aside the question of whether an offer to continue living with one's enslavers might be desirable or amounts to restitution, $200 a week is hardly sufficient compensation for the housework she continued to perform for his family in Seattle. As advocated by the National Domestic Workers Alliance, domestic workers deserve payment for each hour they are required to be in a home. Considering that a well-paid live-in domestic worker in a city like Seattle could have earned as much as $3,000 per month, $200 per week or $800 per month amounts to massive wage theft.

We'll never know how Pulido really felt about her situation. Since her enslavers cannot give us an objective perspective, I decided to turn to her other relatives: a distant cousin in New Jersey; a niece in her hometown of Mayantoc, Tarlac; and the grandchildren of her siblings in the Philippines. I am glad I did. For them, Tizon was no hero. Based on the little knowledge they were able to gather from regular phone calls that Pulido made to her niece in Mayantoc, they do not believe that Pulido lived a good life with Tizon after Leticia's death. They claim Tizon still expected Pulido to work for him. They point to her ongoing childcare duties, saying that Pulido ran an "informal daycare center" in Tizon's home, where she took care of not only Tizon's children but his nieces and nephews as well. This suggests that, as would have been predicted by Patterson, manumission did not take place for Pulido. Tizon and his family continued to "invariably gain" from Pulido despite the change in her status.

How did Tizon justify his continued subjugation of Pulido? Perhaps we can see the answer in his essay, where he often described Pulido as a member of the family. After all, family works for love, not money. Rather than some kind of culturally specific debt-based arrangement, Pulido was entrapped in a culturally specific kin-based servitude, with family abuse fueling her enslavement.

Most of Pulido's family remains in Mayantoc, an agriculture-based municipality in the northern province of Tarlac nestled in the foothills of the Zambales Mountains. Pulido's family resides deep in a valley that can be reached only by crossing a depleted river amid arid land, brown foliage, and glimpses of starved cows and goats. There are no industrial or service jobs to be had in Mayantoc, so most families rely on the land to survive. Pulido's family works as sharecroppers farming rice in the outskirts of town, where the narrow and winding unpaved roads remain unnamed and people distinguish houses by the last names of occupants as opposed to street numbers. Multiple generations of Pulido's extended family reside in a small unpainted bungalow on a small plot of land, where Pulido likewise stayed when visiting from the United States. This house, which I visited one early Sunday morning, is dark and hidden behind other homes away from the road. Behind the house were acres of uncropped land, which I learned Pulido's family depended on for survival—or they did before years of recent drought made farming difficult. Inescapable heat pierced the tinted windows of the car the day we arrived.

A friend and I hired a car to drive three hours to Mayantoc from Manila on roads that grew narrower and narrower the farther we went from the capital. We drove another hour to find Pulido's *barangay*, or local district. Despite the story's widespread coverage in the United States and elsewhere in the Philippines, most people in Mayantoc were not familiar with Pulido's story. We followed complicated directions from store vendors at the central market, officers at the police station, and 2 of 24 barangay captains. None of them knew Pulido, but one of the barangay captains thought to direct us to the poorest district in town, where we eventually found ourselves at the doorstep of Pulido's ancestral home.

Reporters had been reaching out to Pulido's relatives since the publication of Tizon's article, so they were not at all surprised to see two strangers at their doorstep. They welcomed us into their home and immediately drew our attention to the shrine they maintained for their relative, whom they knew as Lola Cosiang. Framed black-and-white pictures, one of Pulido as a young child and another as a much older woman, adorned the only bookshelf in their sparsely furnished living room. The prominence of these pictures reflected how Pulido was and is loved by her family.

Pulido was never supposed to be an unpaid worker. According to her family, Pulido expected to earn a wage from Leticia that would have then allowed her to send money to her parents in Mayantoc. In Tizon's story, Pulido herself makes the decision to come to the United States based on the admittedly false promise of an allowance that she can send to her parents. Unmentioned is the fact that Pulido's parents also had some say. They agreed to have her accompany Leticia and her family to the United States, wrongfully assuming she was going to be a migrant worker, someone who would be able to send remittances regularly and provide for them and other members of her family in the Philippines. Because Pulido never did get paid, she was not able to fulfill this cultural obligation.

Neither of Pulido's parents knew she was enslaved. None of her family did. Leticia and her husband severed Pulido's communication with kin in the Philippines. They denied her the opportunity to visit them and minimized their correspondence. Pulido's parents assumed she had abandoned them. By some accounts, Pulido's father was bitter and resentful about this for the rest of his life. He sent her numerous letters over the years, all unanswered, asking for help from the daughter he assumed was thriving in the United States. He died without learning her true condition. It is clear, even from Tizon's story, that this situation was incredibly difficult for Pulido. When her parents grew ill in the 1970s, she asked to visit them. "Both times she wanted desperately to go home. Both times my parents said 'Sorry.' No money, no time." This refusal devastated Pulido: "After each of her parents died, Lola was sullen and silent for months."

The term for this kind of severing of family ties is "natal alienation," which Patterson and others consider an intrinsic part of the experience of slavery. Pulido was not given the chance to describe this feeling for herself, but the experience of other domestic workers can give us some insight. When asked to describe what it had been like when employers denied their request to do things like pay their final respects to their parents, domestic workers would uniformly reply, "*Masakit*," which in Filipino refers to a deep-seated sorrow and anguish.

Pulido never disclosed to anyone in her family in the Philippines the reason she was never able to visit. Even Pulido's closest living relative, her niece Lolita "Ebia" Pulido-Gabertan, or Nana Ebia, was kept in the dark. The two had known each other as children. In fact, when she was 12 years old, Nana Ebia worked alongside Pulido in the Tizon household. Pulido begged Nana Ebia to leave Mayantoc and follow her to Manila so she could help care for Leticia's newborn baby—Alex Tizon.

Nana Ebia is now in her 70s. Small, frail, and wrinkled beyond her age, she squinted as she spoke. According to Nana Ebia, she had not been compensated for her work with the Tizons. They also beat her and expected her to work at all hours. Nana Ebia had not been indebted to the Tizons in any way and yet she was still subjected to cruel and slave-like conditions. Soon after arriving, she decided to run away. She left with no money, just a *bayong*, a native bag made of woven leaves, and her *bakya*, open-toed wooden clogs commonly used in the Philippines. She walked for hours to the northern bus station in Manila, where she then hitched a ride home to Tarlac.

When Pulido visited Mayantoc for the first time in 1989, Nana Ebia could tell that Pulido had been exploited. According to Nana Ebia, Pulido never talked about her situation in the United States, but Nana Ebia suspected something was wrong because of her worn-out clothing and limited means despite years in the United States. Most telling of all, Pulido had come home without the customary *pasalubong*, a Filipino tradition of travelers returning home with gifts for friends and family. As Nana Ebia wryly observed, "Even people returning from Saudi Arabia come home with chocolates." Nana Ebia only learned the truth of Pulido's enslavement from the article in *The Atlantic*.

Nana Ebia may have escaped servitude in the Tizon household, but Pulido would have found escape more difficult. She was bound not by debt but instead by filial responsibility and cultural obligation. According to Nana Ebia, Pulido saw herself not as a "marginal" or distant relative but as close kin with Leticia. Tizon's grandmother, Leticia's mother, had been Pulido's mother's first cousin. In the United States, Leticia and Pulido would have been considered second cousins.

Reconstructing the timeline offers some clarity. Leticia's mother had died when Leticia was still a child. We can imagine that Tizon's widowed grandfather, Tomas Asuncion, could not care for his daughter on his own and so he asked his deceased wife's family for help. One of his late wife's cousins presented her daughter, who at 18 years old found herself obligated to care for her then-12-year-old cousin. At first, she cared for her cousin's family in Mayantoc. Then she found herself having to relocate to Manila when this cousin was admitted to medical school.

At that time, Pulido could have turned her back on her cousin, but she decided to come along according to Nana Ebia because she was told that she would be paid a wage once in Manila. She was not, yet she stayed. Why? We will never know. Cultural defenders of slavery would say it was because she was bound by debt. Gender scholars would say it was because she was trapped by familial obligation and the ideology of female domesticity.

Another explanation may be found in fresh family trauma. According to Tizon, Tomas Asuncion "had long been haunted by demons, and in 1951 he silenced them with a .32-caliber slug to his temple." This happened not long after Pulido moved to Manila. By then Leticia was married and could arguably rely on her husband for care. Yet Tomas's unfortunate death would have thwarted any plans Pulido might have had to leave. As close kin, how could she abandon Leticia in the wake of her father's suicide? How could she be so callous as to demand a wage from a grieving cousin?

Pulido's enslavement did not happen in a vacuum. In the Philippines, a culture of servitude exists whereby poor people send their children, usually young adolescents, in particular girls, to work in the households of wealthier relatives. A social contract guides this practice. Parents are not necessarily paying off a debt or giving their children away when they agree to this arrangement. This practice is more akin to a barter and trade relationship in which the provision of service would be recognized with some form of investment in the child's education. Similar practices have been documented among young domestic workers in Brazil, Cameroon, Ghana, and Haiti. Families participate not simply for survival but because it can offer an avenue for mobility that would otherwise not be available. To the extent that Pulido's fate can be blamed on this practice, her experience serves as an example of its violation.

Instead of receiving support or education for her years of unpaid labor, Pulido's presence enabled her cousin to complete high school, college, and medical school. She freed her cousin Leticia of childcare. In the United States, Tizon acknowledged, "While she looked after us, my parents went to school and earned advanced degrees." Yet Leticia ultimately reneged on her cultural obligation to reciprocate for her older cousin's years of unpaid labor. She denied Pulido both a salary and an education; the Tizon family kept Pulido illiterate and unpaid.

Tizon suggests that his parents were not entirely to blame, as the Tizons often could not afford to pay Pulido. The family struggled financially in the United States. Tizon shared that his parents had "fancy diplomas but no jobs"; they moved constantly. His parents' high level of educational attainment hid their financial precarity; his mother had to work multiple shifts in the hospital while his father, a lawyer in the Philippines, was constantly unemployed once in the United States. Yet their financial struggles are no excuse for denying Pulido, or any worker, financial compensation.

If Filipino cultural norms are to blame for Pulido's abuse, we can also attribute it to gender and the burden of care imposed on women in the family. Pulido's situation, as kin entrapped by cultural obligation to care for a cousin, follows a pattern I have documented among families in the Philippines. Many parents, both fathers and mothers, leave their children to become temporary migrant laborers. An estimated 25 percent of children in the Philippines have at least one parent working outside the country. Mothers who migrated for work usually left their children under the care of female relatives, some close, such as a sister, and others distant, such as a second cousin. The length of one's absence would vary, with most returning for one month every two years, and some, usually undocumented workers, not returning at all. Like Leticia, who was also missing a parent due to different circumstances, the children of migrant workers relied on extended kin for care.

In families with migrant parents, it is women who find themselves saddled with the day-to-day responsibility of caring for the children left behind. While most migrant men can rely on a female partner to care for their children, the same cannot be said of migrant women with male partners. Instead, they must depend on other women or, as sociologist Joanna Dreby observed in Mexico, on "middlewomen." Like Pulido, these "middlewomen" are often not paid for their labor. They are expected to provide care out of familial obligation. Many told me that not caring for the children of their migrant daughter, sister, sister-in-law, cousin, aunt, or mother would be immoral.

The women I met doing this work rarely received financial compensation and often resented the obligation. Often the migrant mothers would send remittances not to the female caregivers but instead to the oldest child under their watch. Sometimes the recipient of these funds was as young as 12 years old. This meant the caregiver was often short of funds. The abundance of "other mothers" in the Philippines tells us that Pulido's initial experience is not an exception. It fits a pattern of exploitation of one family member by another in the intimate space of the household.

THE ENSLAVEMENT OF EUDOCIA PULIDO caused a scandal in the United States, in part because we assume modern-day slavery does not happen here. Statistics support this assumption, in part. According to the ILO, slavery is more common outside the West, with the greatest likelihood of its occurrence in Asia. But the United States is not immune to the possibility of modern slavery. There are many victims of forced labor in the United States, which includes situations where employers choose to pay workers less than minimum wage, deny overtime pay, and arbitrarily add to their workload. This is especially true for the estimated two million domestic workers in this country.

According to the anti-trafficking organization Polaris Project, domestic workers constitute the largest group of labor-trafficking victims in the United States. Between 2007 and 2017, domestic workers represented 23 percent of approximately 8,000 cases of labor trafficking reported to the National Human Trafficking Hotline. Most victims, about 92 percent, are foreign nationals. The largest group comes from the Philippines (where migrants perform domestic work in large numbers), followed by Mexico. Many victims were trafficked to the United States by employers from Gulf Cooperation Council countries, including the Kingdom of Saudi Arabia, Qatar, Kuwait, and United Arab Emirates. Some were trafficked by Americans, including expatriates returning home for short visits.

The enslavement of domestic workers can happen in the United States for several reasons. First, domestic labor is hidden in the home, which obscures the exploitative behavior of employers, who can easily overwork, underpay, mistreat, and isolate employees in private without facing social or legal penalty. Regulating and enforcing the law in private households is extremely challenging. Within the home, employers often ignore local labor laws and determine employment conditions, including salaries, based on prevailing standards elsewhere.

My own family is not free of fault. I have cousins who paid live-in domestic workers less than minimum wage. The rest of the family discusses this kind of mistreatment, but admittedly we tolerate their misdeeds; our moral outrage is largely contained to raised eyebrows and whisperings at the dinner table during family get-togethers. One distant relative, a nurse who migrated to the United States in the 1980s, compensated a full-time live-in domestic worker whose visa she sponsored from the Philippines only $500 a month, while another, also employed in the medical field, paid an undocumented live-in domestic worker only $1,000 a month. The employee paid $500 a month was poorly treated as well—denied a day off, forced to split a hamburger with her boss's five-year-old daughter when visiting McDonald's, and reprimanded if seen talking to someone else, as she is expected to give her full attention to the daughter. I was not surprised to hear that this domestic worker eventually ran away. The worker who earned more was supposedly treated much better, though they likewise did not have a day off.

I am certain neither of my relatives finds fault in their actions. In fact, they have long encouraged me to hire a domestic worker from the Philippines, whether one whose migration I sponsor or one already in the United States and in desperate need of employment after overstaying their tourist visa. Paying them less than minimum wage, I was told, would be a win-win for both me and the worker, who would be earning much less if they stayed in the Philippines. There are many domestic workers like those mistreated by my relatives. Their experience might not be as extreme as those of Pulido's, but they nevertheless are similar.

Within the American immigration system, two problems, often overlapping, make migrant domestic employees especially vulnerable to abuse. Pulido had been subject to both. The first is a legal regime that subjects temporary labor migrants to indenture, or what Bales refers to as "contract slavery." Pulido initially entered the country legally as a paid household worker under the Tizons' sponsorship in 1964. Tizon's father had been offered a diplomatic appointment in the Philippine foreign services, which qualified him to bring one domestic worker to the United States as part of his household. The domestic worker would be given legal status for three years, which they would then be able to extend for two years but not permanently. This type of visa, the equivalent of which today would be an A-3 visa, restricts the employment of the domestic worker to their sponsor and expires once the diplomatic appointment of the sponsor ends. The worker is indentured because they can work only for their sponsor and have little recourse if the sponsor offers poor working conditions or abuses them.

Other visas that subject migrant domestic workers to a relationship of indenture to their sponsor include the B-1, which is granted to foreigners accompanying employers for short visits, often as tourists, to the United States; the G-5, which is reserved for household employees of officials for international organizations such as the World Bank; and the au pair visa.

Visitors to the United States who sponsor domestic workers usually return to their home countries and bring their staff back with them. These visitors could be tourists, diplomats, or expatriate Americans. But in the 1960s and 1970s a shortage of medical professionals in the United States opened the door for foreign-trained medical professionals such as Leticia Tizon to enter and stay in the country legally as labor migrants. This allowed the Tizon household to switch from having "nonimmigrant visas" to "immigrant visas." The new legal residency of Leticia as a professional with an immigrant visa automatically extended to her dependents but not to household employees. Someone like Pulido would be left ineligible, which explains why she became "illegal" in 1969 when the Tizons became legal permanent residents. For the next 17 years she lived as an undocumented person in the Tizons' home, until the Immigration Reform and Control Act of 1986 offered amnesty and a pathway to legal permanent residency.

During those 17 years, she was subjected to a second systemic problem that enables abuse: the criminalization of undocumented workers. While domestic workers, especially undocumented workers, generally have little recourse to report abuse, hotlines now exist to report illegal or abusive working conditions. This was not the case when Pulido worked for Tizon. Even now, not every domestic worker knows about them, and even if they did, they are not necessarily going to call. This is the case for Joana, a live-in caregiver who makes just $6 an hour working in a six-bed residential facility for the elderly in Los Angeles, significantly less than the minimum wage. Joana knows this. She also knows that her co-workers earn more than double her wage, but she is afraid to complain due to her undocumented status. Researcher Denise Brennan argues that the criminalization of undocumented employees like Joana allows American employers to ignore basic labor standards and makes workers vulnerable, as they must tolerate mistreatment to avoid the risk of deportation.

As an undocumented worker, Joana is forced to tolerate her "bad experiences" with clients and accept her abuse as an unavoidable cost of having "the opportunity to work" and the ability to "send money to the Philippines." In other words, Joana sees abuse as going together with domestic work in the United States. *Tiis*, a Tagalog phrase that means "one must endure," is advice she frequently gives other domestic workers who complain about their mistreatment at work.

Seen in this light, Pulido's subjugation (and Joana's) is not an aberration. It is a result of the systems that render undocumented domestic workers vulnerable to abuse in the United States. Their plight is one shared by other migrant workers toiling in private households in this country. This includes Fedelina Lugasan, who at 82 years old was rescued by the FBI from the home of 79-year-old Benedicta Cox in Northridge, a suburb of Los Angeles. According to news reports, a nurse at a nearby hospital reported her suspicions of human trafficking after a frail Lugasan had begged her for food only to vomit and faint after eating it. Lugasan had been enslaved by Cox for 65 years. For this crime, Cox received 5 years of house arrest and was made to pay $101,119 in restitution. She was spared a more severe penalty because of her old age and poor health. Cox died at the age of 80 while under house arrest. There is also the case of Irma Martinez, a woman from the Philippines enslaved by Jefferson Calimlim and his wife, Elnora, former medical doctors in the Milwaukee area. Like Pulido, Martinez worked from 6 a.m. to 11 p.m. daily for 19 years and could not leave the house unsupervised. The FBI learned of the Calimlims from an anonymous call made to the national hotline of Homeland Security Investigations in 2004. The Calimlims were eventually arrested, sentenced to a federal prison for six years, and then deported back to the Philippines. They were also forced to pay more than $900,000 in restitution to Martinez.

Domestic enslavement is not just a problem in the Filipino migrant community. We see cases of Egyptians, Indians, Indonesians, Mexicans, and many more migrant ethnic groups in the United States subjecting co-ethnics to modern-day slavery. Often employers promise workers a shot at the American dream, only to abuse them once they arrive in the United States. Take the case of Egyptians Abdel Nassar Eid Youssef Ibrahim and his ex-wife, Amal Ahmed Ewis-abd Motelib, who enslaved another Egyptian, Shyima Hall, in Irvine, California. There is also the more gruesome case of Sandra Luz Bearden, a Mexican national, who forced a 12-year-old co-national into domestic servitude and subjected her to terrible treatment. In this case, the "girl spent each morning cleaning the home" and was "taken outside, chained, bound and left with no food or water" after she completed her work.

While domestic enslavement can be a problem of co-ethnic exploitation, the urge to traffic or abuse employees is not intrinsic to any particular culture. Research shows that most co-ethnics readily assist others to succeed in the United States. This was the case, for example, among the Cubans studied by sociologist Alejandro Portes. He documents how pioneer Cuban migrants in Miami helped newer migrants not only adjust but succeed in the United States by showing them how to open and operate a small business. Cultural solidarity and migrant networks helped members of this community overcome the challenges of starting over in the United States. But co-ethnics, as we saw with Farah's trafficker or Tizon's mother, often have access to people vulnerable to trafficking and abuse. Some take advantage and get away with it, and some do not.

The Tizon family got away with it. Unlike Cox and the Calimlims, the Tizons managed to avoid punishment. They were spared arrest and deportation. They were not forced to give Pulido restitution. They were not held accountable. And they did not set her free.

DEFENDERS OF THE TIZON family have often questioned one aspect of Pulido's story. Why didn't she run away, complain to a neighbor, or alert the police? Why didn't she liberate herself, and return to her family in the Philippines after Leticia's passing? They insist that her staying proves she was not really a slave, not subjected to the abysmal conditions we associate with *real* slavery. She was, they say, just poor kin rescued from debt by benevolent relatives. Perhaps she was even content.

But the appearance of contentment cannot be a justification for slavery. As the emancipated man and abolitionist Frederick Douglass tells us: "I have observed this in my experience of slavery, that whenever my condition was improved, instead of its increasing my contentment, it only increased my desire to be free, and set me to thinking of plans to gain my freedom." Abuse victims do not stay because their situation is tolerable. They stay because it is hard to leave one's abuser. Pulido was a slave, and the conditions of her enslavement prevented her from leaving and fulfilling her ultimate goal of reuniting with her "real" family in the Philippines. Three key conditions that made her stay were fear of the unknown, material destitution, and emotional entrapment.

Migrant workers are made vulnerable by their separation from support networks and family. Often, this isolation imprisons the worker. In the case of Fedelina Lugasan of Northridge, multiple wellness checks from the FBI could not convince her to leave Benedicta Cox. After being enslaved for more than 65 years, she likely wondered: Where will I go? Where will I live? Who will provide me with food and shelter?

We could speculate that Pulido likewise feared the unknown. Upon his mother's death, Tizon had given Pulido two choices: either live with him and his family or return to the Philippines. In his telling, she visited the Philippines only to decide to return home. Tizon suggests that her choice to stay signaled some form of manumission. Pulido made the choice of her own free will, thus absolving him and his household. But when talking to Tizon, her words contained darker notes, an undercurrent of fear: "'Everything was not the same,' she told me as we walked around Mayantoc. The old farms were gone. Her house was gone. Her parents and most of her siblings were gone. Childhood friends, the ones still alive, were like strangers." Perhaps Pulido stayed with the Tizon family only because she felt there was no other place to go.

Pulido's decision reminds me of Marilou Ilagan, a domestic worker I met in Los Angeles in the 1990s. Marilou arrived in the United States in 1972. Like Pulido, she had accompanied a Filipino family that later abused her. For 17 years, Marilou worked long hours, was paid little, and was kept isolated. "I did not know anyone here," she shared. Marilou was not physically shackled, but she might as well have been. "I had no friends. I had no outlet. I could not just go out if I wanted to because I had nowhere to go. So, I had no day off." Kept isolated from family and community, Marilou had few options when the opportunity arose to leave.

Another critical issue for many enslaved domestic workers is financial destitution. With no savings or nondomestic skills and often lacking proper visas or other documentation, staying with one's enslaver is a purely pragmatic decision. Pulido may have chosen to stay with Tizon because she had diabetes and could not afford medical care in the Philippines. Or it might have been the risk of losing her Supplemental Security Income (SSI), a monthly benefit given by the U.S. government to legal residents with limited income. Spending more than 30 days outside the country would make one ineligible. In fact, Nana Ebia shared with a local reporter that Pulido extended her stay in the United States to save and prolong the collection of her SSI. Finally, it might have also been her lack of means to retire elsewhere or the physical challenge for someone of her age to be independent, whether in the Philippines or in the United States.

Marilou was slightly more fortunate than Pulido. Her employers at least paid her $300 per month during her decades of labor. And once they no longer needed her—when their kids, whom Marilou helped raise for nearly 18 years, were grown—they helped her legalize her status after the amnesty passed in 1986 and helped her find another job. Marilou managed to secure a position as a domestic worker in a household that more than quadrupled her salary to $400 per week. Marilou arguably experienced manumission. Asked how she had felt about her new job, Marilou responded, "I felt like my life was beginning. You know what I mean—my life changed. I felt free." This was a freedom Pulido never experienced.

Pulido was also denied reparations. Tizon paid Pulido a small salary after his mother's death, but not nearly enough to cover her basic expenses. He did not even help pay for her phone calls to the Philippines, much less offer restitution for more than 50 years of unpaid labor. He could have, for instance, ensured Pulido's retirement in the Philippines and enabled a reunion with her closest kin, Nana Ebia, by promising to send her monthly remittances. This is something that Pulido deeply wanted, according to Nana Ebia, who shared with me Pulido's plans to build an extension onto their ancestral home where she could live and bake goods to sell in the neighborhood. Pulido was supposedly a skilled baker who was slowly sending back her baking tools to Mayantoc before her sudden death of a heart attack. In fact, Pulido was scheduled to return to the Philippines for good just a month after she died. Sending remittances to one's former domestic worker after she "retires" is not unusual. It is a way for employers to provide a worker with an informal pension. Domestic workers, who earn low wages in the informal sector, are unlikely to have resources for retirement. A survey I conducted for Pilipino Workers Center in Los Angeles found that most domestic workers are unable to retire; some have to work well into their 80s. My findings are supported by a national survey conducted by the National Domestic Workers Alliance, which found that less than 2 percent of domestic workers in the United States receive retirement or pension benefits. In addition, only 9 percent of employers contribute to the Social Security of domestic workers.

Besides isolation and poverty, perhaps the most pernicious force that binds workers to their enslavers is emotional coercion. Tizon died a few months before *The Atlantic* published his article and thus never faced criticism for perhaps his most outrageous claim: that there can be redemption from slavery, that slavery can turn to love.

In a featured article in *People* magazine, Tizon's widow, Melissa Tizon, shared pictures of Pulido smiling and laughing with the family. These images are supposed to convey that Pulido was at worst a happy slave, at best a member of the family. As Melissa noted, "We took her to the Philippines a few times during the last 12 years of her life to see if she wanted to move back there, but she always wanted to come home because she missed everybody here." Albert Tizon, Alex's older brother, maintains that it was not coercion but love that kept Pulido in their household. In an interview for a Philippine newspaper, he said Pulido would consistently tell him when asked why she remained loyal to his family, "Where do I go? I can't leave your mom. I love your mom. I love all of you."

I do not doubt that Pulido felt affection toward the Tizons. Yet we need to ask if that affection amounts to manumission or mitigates their culpability. I would argue that the existence of love is not proof that Pulido's enslavement had ended; on the contrary, it highlights the way certain conditions of slavery persisted. Indeed, love can be a mechanism to deny a slave freedom and contentment.

Genuine feelings of love for one's enslaver do not make one less of a slave. Take the case of Lugasan once again. When she heard that her enslaver, Cox, had passed away, she cried, "I love her." Keep in mind that Lugasan had not received remuneration for her work, had nothing but hand-me-down clothes in her possession when the FBI found her, had to eat separately from the family, and in 65 years had not been given a bedroom. Initially, Lugasan had refused to go with the FBI out of worry for Cox's well-being. It took them at least eight visits before she could be convinced otherwise. "I still didn't want to leave her, because there would be no one watching her," Lugasan shared with reporters. It was only after the FBI told her that Cox's daughter had agreed to take full responsibility for the care of her elderly mother that Lugasan finally decided to leave. Lugasan's response to her rescue tells us that emotional attachments do not nullify domestic abuse. This should be obvious considering the dynamics of domestic abuse, which features similar relationships of unequal power and emotional manipulation.

Love exerts such gravitational force because it is often the only source of dignity for victims of slavery like Pulido. Love counters the indignity of sleeping next to a dog, wearing hand-me-down clothes, eating leftovers, and suffering regular beatings. It cloaks the violence of being ripped from one's family. Love hides the crime of abusers who demand that victims like Pulido displace their love for their own family onto their employers. Tizon saw nothing wrong when he shared, "My parents expected Lola to be as devoted to us kids as she was to them." This was an expectation Tizon seemed to carry as well: "Lola was as devoted to my daughters as she'd been to my siblings and me when we were young." Yet, Tizon never asks, why was Pulido so devoted?

Tizon failed to ask this question because he saw Pulido as a "hallowed figure," that is, someone inhabiting a quasi-spiritual plane in which service gave her life meaning. According to Tizon, "She'd had none of the self-serving ambition that drives most of us, and her willingness to give up everything for the people around her won her our love and utter loyalty." In other words, he believed the love and devotion that Pulido had for them was what "made her life worth living." This extraordinary statement tells us that to have purpose in life, to maintain self-respect and dignity, Pulido needed to maintain devotion and love for her enslavers. In some ways, her psychological survival hinged on maintaining this love, and the loyalty that it earned. But while this love gave her life dignity, it also fueled her enslavement. Via the twisted logic of emotional entrapment, her love for the Tizons meant that she didn't need to get paid, and in their eyes her love exonerated them of wrongdoing.

SLAVERY IS NOT JUST an economic exchange. It's also an experience of entrapment. In many ways, Pulido's life embodies a series of deceptions that the Tizon family deployed to maintain their grip on her. Pulido wanted to earn money for her family, a desire that the Tizon family exploited. She dreamed of having enough to return to and retire in the Philippines, and kept working for the Tizons in pursuit of this dream, while the Tizons ensured her exploitation by maintaining as much as dashing the fulfillment of this dream.

Ever since she was 18 years old, Pulido had been misled with one unfulfilled promise after another and deceived into thinking she was eventually going to be paid by the Tizons. This started with the false promise that she would be paid in Manila. It was followed by yet another lie that she would be paid once in the United States. At some point, she was told she would eventually receive an inheritance big enough to allow her to retire comfortably in the Philippines. That also never materialized. Nana Ebia told the story of how Pulido was made to believe that she would at some point inherit a share of some land in the Philippines that Leticia owned. This share would be payment for all her years of labor. The Tizons did eventually sell the land, but according to Nana Ebia, they reneged on their promise to give Pulido a share of the proceeds. Pulido, she told me, was devastated.

Pulido had many aspirations and not all of them revolved around the Tizons. I spoke to other relatives in Mayantoc besides Nana Ebia, including two younger men who looked to be in their early 20s. They let me know they were "the grandchildren of Lola Cosiang." I knew Pulido had never had children, so I assumed they were the grandchildren of one of her siblings. Given the strength of extended kinship ties in the Philippines, it wasn't odd to hear them express their unequivocal love for their "Lola Cosiang." This is a love they were sure was reciprocated. Despite her meager earnings, Pulido, toward the last years of her life, diligently sent them money every May and December. She sent money in May to help cover school expenses and in December to ensure her family had the means to celebrate Christmas. When she passed, the flow of money stopped. As they told me, so did their schooling. This disruption likely marked the end of mobility for Pulido's family.

After her death, Pulido experienced a final period of natal alienation. For Tizon, Pulido's ashes were an inconvenience. For Pulido's family, they were sacred. Five years passed before Tizon returned Pulido's ashes to the Philippines. Tizon assumed no one cared. Yet many did care. I was told that one uncle had waited for Pulido's remains but died without the opportunity to mourn her properly. Another sibling died waiting as well; they passed away two years after Pulido but three years before Tizon decided to return her remains. Tizon set Pulido apart as a "hallowed figure," devoted to his family, but he was oblivious to the other meaningful relationships in her life.

According to Nana Ebia, Pulido wished to be buried alongside her parents. Tizon ignored this request. To his credit, Tizon did try to give Pulido a proper burial and paid the 35,000 pesos, which is around $667, that it cost to buy a plot at the Eternal Bliss Memorial Park near the central market of Mayantoc. Yet Tizon chose not to relocate Pulido's parents, both of whom had been buried far from town in an "inaccessible mountainous area." To grant Pulido's wish, a distant relative in New Jersey turned to crowdsourcing and raised $2,600 to move her parents' remains to be next to the daughter they lost when she was only 18 years old. Pulido was finally laid to rest in Mayantoc in 2016; years later, her parents were moved beside her.

Why did Tizon finally decide to give Pulido a proper burial? Her relatives suspect he did it not for Pulido's sake but for his own benefit. They think it had something to do with the timing of the publication of his article in *The Atlantic*. It would have looked bad for Tizon, they thought, if the article was published before he gave Pulido a proper burial. The real answer is perhaps even more cynical. The experience of bringing the ashes to the Philippines for burial provided Tizon with scenes of emotional closure for the article, a tidy conclusion to a narrative arc in which Tizon seeks redemption and forgiveness for himself and his family for exploiting a person for decades as a modern-day slave.

CHAPTER 2

THE RISKS MIGRANTS TAKE

—

"KAYA MO BA?" the instructor asks. "Can you take it?"

I am sitting in a classroom in a dark, damp, and aging government building in Manila, the capital of the Philippines. The hallways are ill-lit, and the elevators are broken. We were told not to use them anyway. There is no toilet paper in the restrooms and no air-conditioning. White plastic chairs fill almost every inch of the classroom, preventing doors from fully opening, and crowding the participants. Nearly 100 women fill this room, which has a maximum capacity of 60.

The women are attending a seminar for migrant workers headed to the Middle East, during which they will learn about the challenges they are likely to confront there. The women are told that there is a high likelihood that they are going to be not only isolated, overworked, and called derogatory names by employers but also raped. The word "rape" is met with gasps and widened eyes. Whispers echo around the room. The instructor then shares vivid stories of sexual assault. An employer greeting a domestic worker with their naked body, another placing their erect penis on the domestic worker's shoulder, or an employer forcibly fondling breasts are just some of the examples.*

"Kaya para sa pamilya?" the instructor asks again. "Can we take it for the family?"

The instructor then cues the desired response. "Kaya," the women say. "We can."

ON ANY TYPICAL WEEKDAY morning, some 3,000 prospective migrant domestic workers might crowd the streets of Manila waiting for the government offices of the Overseas Workers Welfare Administration to open so they might attend these mandatory seminars. Some travel for 10 hours on the road; others take a three-day boat ride. Hardly anyone is local to the National Capital Region, which like Los Angeles or New York is far too expensive for most migrant workers. As one of the largest source countries of migrant domestic workers, second only to Indonesia, the Philippines looks out for the welfare of its citizens by carefully managing their out-migration. Before they can exit the country, each migrant must complete a seminar that not only acculturates them to their destination but also forewarns them of the challenges they may face once there. In the case of domestic workers, the challenges are plenty: loneliness, isolation, wage theft, abuse, and as described earlier, even rape. The Philippines runs these seminars to ensure that migrant workers are prepared to face the worst-case scenario.

The Philippine state describes migrant domestic work as a

---

* I sat through a hundred hours of these seminars. These examples were not all mentioned in a single seminar; I gathered them here for effect. But none is fabricated. They reflect real-life experiences of former migrants from the Philippines.

"highly vulnerable occupation." This raises the question of why prospective migrants still pursue it. Scholars have argued that migrants are unaware of the risks. According to Dutch legal scholar Antoinette Vlieger, who researches domestic workers in the Kingdom of Saudi Arabia and United Arab Emirates, recruitment agents deceive and misinform prospective migrants about their labor conditions. American anthropologist Andrew Gardner agrees. He writes on South Asian construction workers in Bahrain and Qatar. He claims that migrant returnees who fare poorly hide their past experiences out of shame. This leaves poor villagers aware of only the successes of migration from triumphant returnees who can pay off their debt, buy land, and start businesses.

Yet, as I learned by observing these mandatory seminars, migrant domestic workers are fully aware of the perils of migration. Sending states like the Philippines, Ethiopia, Indonesia, and Sri Lanka make sure of it. Migrant domestic workers from these countries cannot leave without first completing a government-mandated predeparture orientation seminar like the ones I attended in Manila. In the Philippines, the government administers these seminars almost daily. Varying in length according to destination, they last from one to six days. They are intended to prepare migrant domestic workers for their lives overseas, providing rudimentary language training, culture-familiarization lessons, and stress-management training.

These seminars teach migrants that forced labor, meaning the involuntary performance of a job under threat of penalty, is the norm. By the time they attend the seminar, participants have already signed a two-year contract, so quitting is not an option. After participants are informed that they will likely be subjected to rape, they are then encouraged to develop strategies of deflection. To not look male employers in the eye and to limit their interactions to the women in the household. Ultimately, they are told to develop grit. In class after class I heard the harrowing call and response of "Kaya mo ba?" and "Kaya." Drilling attendees in consent to slave-like conditions is a goal of these seminars. Forewarning migrants of the dangers of labor migration allows the Philippines to avoid accountability by transferring it to the individuals who migrate.

For the most part, migrants are not headed to the West. A handful of them migrate to the United States, but few have the means or the resources to do so. Unless an employer sponsors their visa (as the Tizon family did for Pulido), a migrant would need to enter the country on a tourist visa, which is nearly impossible to obtain without a sizable bank account, businesses, or properties. Instead, domestic workers go to destinations that are more generous in their provision of work visas: Hong Kong, Kuwait, Israel, Singapore, United Arab Emirates, to name a few. Canada and Denmark are two notable exceptions of Western nations with slightly lower bars to entry. Labor-recruitment agencies funnel migrants to jobs across the globe. In the Philippines alone, there are more than 800 of these agencies.

Many migrant domestic workers choose to work in the Middle East, where employers are expected to pay for the cost of their migration, including visa fees, airfare, and labor-recruitment agency fees. This region is home to 27 percent of all migrant workers globally. Middle Eastern countries are also more accessible for migrants because they don't hold any education requirements. In most other destinations, domestic workers need at least a high school degree to pursue domestic work.

From my more than two decades of research on migrant women workers in Europe, Asia, and North America, I have come to learn that migrant workers are usually informed of the risks and make rational, price-sensitive decisions about entering into migrant labor contracts. Yet the hundreds of people I have studied also categorically fit the definition of forced-labor and human-trafficking victims. My research shows that victims put themselves at risk of exploitation because their other choice is deep poverty or even starvation and death. They choose migration, despite all its risks, because it gives them hope.

This chapter attempts to describe the experience of being a migrant worker in two common destinations, Dubai and Singapore, and how the structures of migrant labor put individuals at risk of forced labor and human trafficking.

BETWEEN 2014 AND 2016, I interviewed over 85 domestic workers who had migrated from the Philippines to Dubai, trying to understand why they would put themselves at risk to pursue migrant work and to learn what they experienced once there. One of the most harrowing stories I heard came from a woman named Nada, whose name means "nothing" not only in Spanish but also in the woman's dialect of Chavacano, a Spanish-based creole language spoken in the southern region of the Philippines. At 50 years old, Nada was older than other domestic workers, who mostly called her "Tita," which means "aunt" in the Philippines. At a certain point, she adopted this name for herself, so that's what I'll call her here.

Tita was from a remote underdeveloped area in the mountains of the southern island of Basilan in the Autonomous Region in Muslim Mindanao, an area recently renamed Bangsamoro by the government in reference to it being a "nation of the Moros." Basilan is best known as the headquarters of the Al Qaeda–linked terrorist group Abu Sayyaf. Tita was raised in dire poverty, which probably explained her frail physique and short stature. She was no more than 4 feet, 10 inches tall. During my many visits to her apartment in Dubai, Tita told me stories of her childhood. Many were unpleasant. She would describe how her family was often left unhoused by the frequent cross fire between Moro Muslim rebels and the Philippine military. Her home was a modest nipa hut made of wood with a thatched roof; it ignited easily. Each side burned down her house at least once. Yet this was not the worst of her experiences. When she was just 13 years old, a neighbor raped and impregnated her. Then she was forced to marry him because not doing so would have embarrassed her clan.

Tita ended up bearing two children with her rapist, who was also a domestic abuser. He was almost never around and when he was, he beat Tita and failed to provide for the family. Most days, Tita and her children had nothing to eat but the cassava that grew near her home. For Tita, the worst of her struggles came when her children got sick and she worried that she would not have the means to care for them. One of her children died of sepsis because she could not afford antibiotics. Tita decided to become a migrant domestic worker because she could not bear the pain of seeing another loved one die another preventable death.

She worked stints in Kuwait and the Kingdom of Saudi Arabia before coming to the United Arab Emirates. Each time Tita left the Philippines, she had to rely on a fixer to process her migration. A fixer is someone, usually a former migrant worker, who is paid by a recruitment agency to personally escort prospective migrant workers from remote, impoverished villages to the recruitment office in Manila. For their services, fixers usually receive the equivalent of at least a month of their client's future wages. Tita told me that she relied on a fixer because she would not otherwise have known how to secure a job abroad. Having completed school only through the fifth grade, she did not trust herself to figure out how to do so.

Tita did not always fare well abroad. While she held fond memories of her many years in Jeddah, Saudi Arabia, other places were a struggle. Migrants such as Tita, who rely on recruitment agencies to process their labor migration, are beholden to whatever job the agency might assign them. They don't pick their destination or their employer. This diminished autonomy leaves migrant workers vulnerable to abuse. In Kuwait, her first country of employment, Tita was sexually assaulted. She then endured forced starvation in the emirate of Fujairah. Her employers gave her a piece of *kuboos*, pita bread, for breakfast, one piece of egg and a cup of rice for lunch, and whatever might be leftover from dinner. Despite these dismal working conditions, Tita agreed to extend her contract with the family in Fujairah. The security of employment for another two years was better than the threat of unemployment. But when Tita developed cataracts, her employers in Fujairah didn't want to pay for the expenses that health insurance would not cover for eye surgery. They opted to deport Tita instead.

By the time I met Tita, she had become an "unauthorized" worker. At the airport, Tita managed to escape and make her way to one of the working-class districts in Old Dubai, where she lasted three months doing part-time childcare for middle-class Filipinos. Then the Criminal Investigation Department raided Tita's apartment. She was incarcerated and eventually deported back to the

Philippines. After nearly two decades of domestic work abroad, Tita returned to Basilan without any savings. Tragically, Tita got sick not long after returning to Basilan and died from sepsis for which she could not afford medication.

How unusual is Tita's experience? Though admittedly extreme, Tita's story resonates with those of hundreds of women I have met in my decades of research. From the Filipino women in the Manila seminars to the South Asian workers who risked debt and indenture to construct buildings for the 2022 World Cup in Qatar, to Myanmar nationals who agreed to work under slave-like conditions in Thai fishing boats, migrants risk harm for the hope of economic survival. Tita sought this escape multiple times. As Anna Triandafyllidou observes of irregular migrants in Greece, the "hopeful uncertainty" of migration was better than the "hopeless certainty" of Tita's poverty in the Philippines.

I ENCOUNTERED SANAYA, a Sri Lankan migrant, as she was coming up on a year in the employment of an American family in Dubai. When deciding to migrate, Sanaya had not been deterred by news stories in Sri Lanka about the trafficking of migrant domestic workers in the United Arab Emirates, including stories of domestic workers jumping to their deaths to escape abusive employers. Sanaya's husband had already migrated—he worked at a food-processing plant in Dubai—but his salary barely covered their family's daily expenses in Sri Lanka, and she needed a solution to her family's compounding debt. Having a husband abroad did help, though. Unlike Tita and others, Sanaya could lower her risks by avoiding a costly labor-recruitment agency, and she had the means to cover her own airfare and a United Arab Emirates tourist visa. UAE employers often cover the costs of a worker's migration and then defray those costs by paying the migrant lower wages. Sanaya hoped that by covering the costs of her own migration she might secure a more competitive salary.

Once in Dubai, Sanaya began to look for an employer by asking friends, acquaintances, and even strangers for referrals. She also scoured the classified ads on a popular website, dubizzle.com, and searched bulletin boards in local supermarkets. Sanaya's search was urgent. Each day she failed to find work she incurred costs for food and lodging. Because her husband lived in a dormitory restricted to men, Sanaya had to rent a bedspace in the apartment of an acquaintance. Desperate to secure a job before her visa lapsed, Sanaya answered more than a dozen ads, but only one person scheduled an interview and offered her a job. Without other prospects, Sanaya felt she had to accept their terms, which were dismal. Less than a year into the job, Sanaya already wanted to quit.

Sanaya's employer is a white woman named Irene. Born and raised in Portland, Irene has lived in the city-state of Dubai for more than a decade. Located off the Arabian Gulf in the United Arab Emirates, Dubai boasts luxury shopping, opulent hotels, gastronomic delights, a vibrant nightlife, and, for expatriate residents, high salaries and low taxes. Irene is one of an estimated 50,000 Americans living in Dubai. After graduating from college in the Northwest, she secured a job in the tech industry and did quite well from the rapid rise in her company's stock. She relocated to Paris, went to culinary school, met her North African husband, and then followed him to Dubai. While her husband, an executive for a multinational company, travels across the region for work, Irene stays home and takes care of their three school-age children.

Irene keeps busy by staying entrepreneurial. She manages rental properties in the United States and Europe. Irene looks like a typical suburban housewife from Oregon. She avoids makeup, always ties her hair back in a ponytail, and dresses simply in a T-shirt and yoga pants. She downplays her appearance so as not to call attention to her wealth. Irene resides in a spacious villa in Jumeirah, an exclusive neighborhood in Dubai with an adjacent beach, a sailing club, upscale restaurants, and high-end retail stores. Rents in this neighborhood are high, upwards of $5,000 per month.

Irene employs a domestic worker because it is affordable. As she admits, "It's much less expensive here than it will be anyplace else we probably will live." In a country without a minimum wage, domestic workers in the United Arab Emirates can earn as little as $150 per month. Irene pays more, giving Sanaya a monthly salary of $400. In exchange, Sanaya frees Irene of the mundane tasks of running her household, from "nagging at the kids to pick up crumbs and spills" to the daily housework of washing dishes and dusting furniture. Sanaya is always there to "come in and clean up." Every day, Sanaya vacuums, mops, dusts, disinfects, and washes anything from windows to dishes to the clothes worn by Irene's family. Considering she works at least 12 hours per day for six days a week, Sanaya averages the measly hourly rate of less than $1.40.

Sanaya's $400 monthly salary, while not rock bottom, is 60 percent lower than the $1,000 monthly rate that other well-to-do employers in the neighborhood pay domestic workers and 20 percent less than the $500 recommended in online American expatriate community forums. Still, Irene insists that she pays Sanaya adequately, pointing out how she also provides her with basic food staples like bread and rice and covers the annual costs of both her residence visa, which is $1,350, and health insurance, which costs anywhere from $1,350 to $2,700. These provisions are mandatory expenses for domestic employers, and do not necessarily make Irene more humanitarian or generous than other employers.

Sanaya knows this, which is why she wants to work for someone else. But she cannot switch employers without Irene's permission, and Irene refuses to let her go. Releasing Sanaya from her labor contract would be a costly inconvenience for Irene. Hiring a new person would require her to pay a recruitment agency fee. This fee could be as high as $3,000 for a domestic worker coming from abroad, given the travel, visa, and recruitment fees. Hiring locally—and there are plenty of domestic workers available locally—is much cheaper, at most $1,000 and potentially as little as $200. The local labor market includes workers who have completed their prior labor contract and been given permission by their employer to find a new job, as well as workers, like Sanaya, who entered the country independently with a tourist visa. Employers can locate them formally through an agency or informally through handwritten postings on supermarket bulletin boards or on dubizzle.com. This is how Irene connected with Sanaya in the first place.

Sanaya is convinced that her overall work conditions would improve in another household. She knows from friends that the labor conditions in Irene's household are poor. In Dubai, employers are contractually obligated to provide domestic workers with food. While some employers fulfill this obligation by sharing meals with domestic workers, others extend a food allowance. Irene does neither. Irene admits to not wanting to be "responsible for her food." She often feeds Sanaya leftovers.

Besides paying low wages and inflicting food deprivation, Irene also restricts Sanaya's freedom. Irene not only cancels Sanaya's weekly day off on a regular basis, she also forbids her from cohabiting with her husband. Irene claims she does this because she believes it is illegal for a domestic worker like Sanaya to get pregnant. This is untrue. However, pregnancy outside of marriage was historically not allowed in the United Arab Emirates. It was only decriminalized in November 2021. Abortion is illegal, resulting in up to one year of imprisonment and a fine of 10,000 dirhams, or $2,722. In the past, employers managed the pregnancy of domestic workers by quietly processing their repatriation. More to the point, a pregnant domestic worker would inconvenience Irene, who expects a lot of work from Sanaya. In addition to her regular responsibilities, which include laundry and ironing, washing dishes, and the intensive cleaning of at least one area of the house daily, Irene demands additional tasks, including gardening, babysitting after hours, and cleaning a rental unit. Irene does not pay Sanaya extra for these previously undisclosed tasks, which is a clear labor offense. Migrant advocates, including the ILO, have constructed a term for it, "contract substitution."

While Tita's story shows how poverty drives individuals to take on the risk of becoming migrant workers—and the potential horrors of sexual abuse—Sanaya's reveals a much more common experience of economic rather than sexual exploitation. And while Dubai and other Middle Eastern destinations are notorious for exploiting migrant laborers with impunity, Sanaya's story also shows us that Western expatriates often exploit workers as well. Demanding uncompensated tasks and refusing a worker's demands to change employers are textbook examples of forced labor. The question, then, is what makes workers like Sanaya and Tita so vulnerable to abuse.

Employment of domestic workers in the United Arab Emirates is governed through what is known as the *kafala* system. This legal regime is a sponsorship system that binds migrant domestic workers to their employers. Under the kafala, domestic workers are indentured to their sponsor—the person who pays for their "maid" visa—as a live-in worker (in rare cases, a worker will opt for live-out employment). Domestic workers are legally prevented from seeking other employment and must secure the permission of their sponsor to transfer jobs or exit the country. Yet employers like Irene dislike granting domestic workers permission to quit, as this forfeits whatever fees they might have paid for visas or to migrant-recruitment agencies. They believe this fee entitles them to at least two years of continuous domestic service regardless of how they treat the worker.

As sponsors, employers have the power to terminate the worker's visa and force their deportation. While sponsors can fire workers at will, domestic workers in Dubai must be able to prove abuse in order to leave; dissatisfaction is not a recognized reason to break their contract. However, the mere presence of abuse does not free domestic workers from the shackles of the kafala. To secure a release from their contract, the worker would need to bring a claim of abuse to the migrant-recruitment agency. Until the claims are verified and their case is upheld, the worker can't work elsewhere. They usually stay in the shelter provided by the recruitment center during this time. On rare occasions employers will release a worker in exchange for dropping the abuse claim. But bringing such a claim is difficult and dangerous. It comes at the risk of their forced exit from the country, as employers can retaliate by canceling their visa, a process that takes less than one day.

The worker may decide to flee an abusive situation and become undocumented, but that carries risks as well. If any domestic worker, including an abused one, quits without permission, they become an "absconder." Absconding is a crime and punishable with incarceration and deportation. Historically, those who quit without permission can avoid incarceration if they manage to seek shelter at either an embassy or a consulate within 48 hours of escape. This, however, does not mean they will be able to reenter the local labor market. Quitting without permission usually results in the "cancellation" of a worker's contract. Even if they are fleeing abuse, the worker cannot seek a new sponsor, and they are repatriated to their country of origin.

The draconian system of the kafala is not exclusive to the United Arab Emirates. Neighboring countries, including other members of the Gulf Cooperation Council such as Kuwait, Oman, and the Kingdom of Saudi Arabia, employ a similar system of governance. In fact, indenture is the norm for migrant domestic workers across the globe, as kafala-like systems also exist for domestic workers in Europe, East Asia, and North America. Italy, due to the strength of labor unions, is one of the only countries that allow migrant domestic workers to work for multiple employers and permit them to maintain their own residence. Most other countries that grant legal residency to migrant domestic workers largely prohibit them from participating in the free market. Instead, they are, like domestic workers in the United Arab Emirates, bound to work solely for their visa sponsor.

In Canada, migrant domestic workers historically entered the country under the Live-In Caregiver Program. Under this program, migrant domestic workers qualified for legal permanent residency only after they had completed two years of continuous live-in employment in one household within four years of their entry to the country. Not surprisingly, abuse was documented there as well. In response to cries of human trafficking, Canada reformed the program in 2014 and eliminated the live-in requirement. Yet abuse persists. In a social media group for Filipinos in Canada, anonymous complaints of long work hours are common. "How do I tell my employer that my work hours are too long? I am a new live-in worker who has been in Canada for months," one post from 2023 asked. Another worker complained that they worked 15 hours a day without overtime compensation because their employers believed that their migration costs—nearly 6,000 Canadian dollars—should be calculated against their future earnings. Charging employees for their migration costs is illegal in Canada, but employers still do this, assuming correctly that indentured employees are unlikely to report them.

The United States is also not exempt from the indenture of migrant domestic workers, as we saw with the situation of au pairs and domestic workers (such as Eudocia Pulido) who accompany diplomats, employees of international organizations such as the World Bank, and tourists or American expatriates visiting for a limited time period. These domestic workers can work only for their visa sponsor. Other democratic countries that subject domestic workers to kafala-like conditions include England, Israel, and Turkey. Various European countries, such as Denmark, Norway, and the Netherlands, have indentured au pair systems. In Denmark, au pairs can change their host family only twice in a two-year period. In Israel, which relies primarily on workers from the Philippines for the care of its elderly, migrant domestic workers can change jobs only three times during their first 63 months of employment. In Southeast Asia, Singapore restricts domestic workers to live-in employment in one household and requires that they secure the permission of their sponsoring employer to change jobs. In Hong Kong, domestic workers who want to quit are bound by the "two-week rule," a law that requires them to secure another employer within two weeks of their termination to avoid deportation. Domestic workers in Turkey and au pairs in the United States face similar time constraints.

Among researchers who study domestic labor, there is a general sentiment that a lack of proper regulation and systems such as the kafala can be described as "structural violence," a term Johan Galtung coined in the 1960s, because these lapses in governance lead to frequent mistreatment of domestic workers, including physical and sexual violence. Substantiating such arguments is the steady flow of runaways in migrant shelters. Shelters operated by the Philippine government in its embassy in Abu Dhabi and consulate in Dubai were often over capacity when I visited them while doing research between 2012 and 2016. Government officials were even forced to convert the reception area of the consulate in Dubai into sleeping quarters at night. I often overheard first-hand accounts from shelter occupants of horrific treatment by employers such as beatings, malnourishment, and overwork.

According to Human Rights Watch, abuse is most likely when the business model of hiring a domestic worker requires the employer to pay an initial fee to labor recruiters, because it gives employers the mindset of having "bought" the domestic worker. This particular dynamic is known as "debt bondage," which I observed closely during 12 noncontinuous months of research in Singapore in 2016 and 2018. Southeast Asia is home to the second-largest number of migrant domestic workers (the Middle East has the most; Europe is third). In Singapore, workers are often required to forfeit their first six months of wages to their employer to pay for the costs of their migration. This arrangement entraps domestic workers and discourages them from quitting. As a domestic worker I met explained, "After six months of a salary deduction, you start to think about how you really do not like your employers. You are debt-free finally and you want to change employers. But you do not know how, but you somehow find the will to stick around. You could wait until you reach two years of working for them. Then it is hard because you paid six months of your salary only to change jobs after two years. You then ask yourself if you are willing to undergo another experience of a salary deduction."

Another domestic worker, Marcy, agreed. Marcy is a college-educated domestic worker whose earnings as an administrative assistant in the Philippines had not been sufficient to sustain her family. An agency in Manila told her she would earn at least 450 Singaporean dollars (S$450), or US$338, per month, but did not mention the salary-deduction system. Once in Singapore, Marcy discovered that she would have to wait seven months for her first paycheck. This was painful. She recalls the distress this caused her: "I feel bad. I feel very upset because . . . I receive monthly $20 allowance for seven months. I cannot send money [to my family] . . . , I was going crazy."

Marcy's experience was made more unbearable by the awful labor conditions she faced. In her first job, her employers paid her S$360, or US$267, instead of their agreed-upon monthly salary of S$450. She was made to work continuously for more than 14 hours each day. It is difficult to imagine how someone could do this much housework in one day, but Marcy swore she did. As Marcy explained, she had to perform deep cleaning not weekly but daily. Her employers demanded she clean the kitchen floor by scrubbing it on her knees—supposedly to remove oil she spilled while cooking—as opposed to using a mop. Also, she was expected to clean two homes and a separate office.

Quitting was never an option for Marcy. She felt doubly entrapped, first by indenture and second by debt. Employed under Singapore's kafala-like system, Marcy was conscious of her employer's power to fire and deport her at will. She feared that she would be deported back to the Philippines before she could earn enough money to offset the hefty agency fee she was charged to go to Singapore. She also didn't want to transfer jobs for fear of adding to her debt.

Domestic workers often find themselves in a lose-lose situation. If the worker cannot tolerate abuse for the entire two-year contract, they are punished with lost wages. This had happened to Marcy's friend Cheros, who quit nine months into her first job because she could no longer tolerate her employers' daily disparagements. Quitting came at a steep cost; she was paid "two months of salary for nine months of work." But tolerating abuse is not necessarily rewarded. Marcy stuck it out with her employers and completed her contract, but when she refused to extend her contract and stay for another two years, they retaliated by canceling her visa. Since she was "canceled" as opposed to "released," she had to exit the country and start her migration process to Singapore all over again. Instead of having to pay only a one-month wage penalty as a "transfer maid" for her second job in Singapore, Marcy had to once again pay agencies in both Singapore and the Philippines a total of six months of her wages for the security of a two-year labor contract.

Employers in Singapore are aware that they "have all the power over the maid," as one employer mentioned in an interview. In most cases, employers abuse their power by controlling an employee's time. They micromanage the worker's tasks and demand work at all hours. They also seize entire days by denying the worker their day off. Most significantly, they might prevent an employee from switching to a new employer, which allows an employer to control months or years of a worker's time.

Dorothy, a wealthy sales consultant, is one such employer. She bans domestic workers from using the phone while working and does not allow them to rest during "work hours," which last from 6 a.m. until 8 p.m. She shared, "I told her, she is not allowed to use the phone when she is working. I told her before she worked for me, I say, 'You cannot take a nap in the afternoon. No sleeping in the afternoon.'" Due to these stringent rules, Dorothy's domestic worker hides in the bathroom to squeeze in a few minutes of rest during her shift. Dorothy complained, "I was like, what is she doing in there. It was quiet. I thought maybe washing clothes, but it was quiet. No, cannot be taking shower, because there is no sound of water. No nothing, and it was quiet. So, I called her, I say, 'What are you doing? Are you sleeping there?' She said no. I said, 'Yes, sleeping.'" This incident did not prompt Dorothy to consider whether she was overworking her domestic worker. Instead, she saw it as a mark of her employee's laziness.

Employers like Dorothy normalize slave-like conditions. A newcomer to Singapore named Albert can attest to this. Albert is a 25-year-old transgender man who migrated to Singapore to support his widowed mother and two younger siblings. His family was unhoused in the Philippines. He can now provide them with a home, but his family's stability has come at the expense of his enslavement.

Albert is clearly a victim of human trafficking. He migrated thinking he would earn S$500 a month, only to learn he would earn no more than S$450. He also mistakenly thought that his salary would be deducted for only six months, not seven and a half. I met Albert at a café behind Lucky Plaza, a mall on Orchard Road that is the hub for Filipino domestic workers on Sundays, their usual day off. Albert gets only two days off per month. Tall and lanky, Albert looked like he was going to cry the entire time we spoke. Across the table, he kept repeating, "I have seven more months until I can transfer employers." He chanted it almost like a mantra. Asked to describe why he found his current employers unbearable, he stared at me and asked, "Where do I start?"

Albert began by describing his bedroom: "Look at my room. My room is so small. I do not have an electric fan. I have been putting up with not having an electric fan for so long. It is so hot. There is no window." Albert wishes he could quit and find a new employer, but he cannot. He has asked for permission to leave but was told he would not be released until he completed his two-year contract, citing the agency fee. Albert was indignant about this, considering that his employers technically had not paid the S$3,375 charged by the agency; *he* had, with his unpaid labor.

As with Marcy, Albert's labor conditions magnified his debt burden. He was overworked, monitored, and ill-fed. He complained, "They are also so cheap when it comes to my food. I am only fed bread in the morning. They live in a three-story house, and I alone have to clean it. Two cars. I alone have to clean them every day. When you tell them you are hungry, they tell you to stop complaining, and ask, why are you always hungry? You think, it is because you only let me eat bread in the morning? Then, they always just serve me instant noodles for lunch. If not instant noodles, then fried rice without any meat. Then at night, they feed me leftovers." When

I asked if he could grab a snack if hungry, Albert responded, "No, they would accuse me of stealing.... I am not allowed to open the refrigerator. It is against the rule to open the refrigerator!"

Albert works an average of 16 hours per day. He must wake up at 5 a.m. and work nearly nonstop until 10 p.m., sometimes even 11 p.m. He is rarely afforded breaks, and those breaks are never longer than 30 minutes. Albert's favorite room in the house is the bathroom. There, he turns on the faucet for 5 minutes and tries to rest. How does Albert power through? He finds hope in the stories of friends such as Pat, a transgender domestic worker who accompanied Albert to the interview. Pat shared how he had finally managed to build a house in the Philippines after having worked in Singapore for six years. Albert aspires to do the same. Albert persists because he refuses to "surrender" to his life of poverty in the Philippines. When speaking about his employers, Albert could not help but sigh, "I really do not know why my employers are the way they are."

Many workers I met in Singapore shared Albert's experience. Another worker, Maryjane, described her first employer in similar ways. They made her work for 21 hours every day, from 5 a.m. until 2 a.m. Describing her situation, Maryjane shared, "I experienced working while closing my eyes for a little bit just so I could rest because I felt like I was going to collapse from exhaustion. The only thing I could do was pray. I would close my eyes for three minutes so I could find strength to keep on working. After working the whole day, the couple would make me give them a massage. This is really what I experienced. It is like they didn't even bother to consider how I have been working the whole day. I would not be done with my work until two o'clock in the morning." Fortunately for Maryjane, this employer allowed her to quit after seven months of what

Maryjane described as a life of sheer hell. She then managed to find a job with much more humane work conditions, which made sacrificing two more months of wages for the agency fee well worth it from her perspective.

A worker named Milagros also managed to escape her contract early, in her case, after nine months. She, too, worked for employers who seemed to think they had purchased a servant's time. She told me, "You work like a horse. We would arrive at the house of my employer's grandparents at 7:00 in the morning and then we would go home at 9:30 at night. The whole day I would be with my one-year-old ward who I cared for 24 hours every day. When we made it back to my employer's home, I would still have to work. I would have to clean, wash the dishes, iron the clothes. The work never ended. Then, the child would wake up. It would be around 11 o'clock at night. I would then have to feed them again. I never got any rest."

Not all employers are like those of Albert, Maryjane, or Milagros. The experience of a worker named Lita was drastically different. A widow who has worked in Singapore for nearly two decades, Lita is given plenty of autonomy running the household of an oil company executive. With a credit card to purchase groceries, she plans the weekly meals of the household on her own. Sometimes Lita seeks input from her employers, asking them if they would like to try a new dish or have her bake their favorite cake. Lita has also established her own cleaning routine. Occasionally her employer will ask Lita to double-check her cleaning but for the most part they leave her alone. She has the time to chat with her three children in the Philippines on Facebook Messenger, and she controls her own work schedule, which is how Lita managed to meet me for coffee in the middle of the day one Wednesday afternoon. When Lita's work is done, she can freely leave her employers' house without permission. Lita might be one of the highest-paid domestic workers in Singapore, receiving a monthly salary of S$1,300. This allows her to comfortably send remittances to her daughters in the Philippines each month.

"It is like being in heaven," Lita responded when asked to describe her work situation. But life hasn't always been rosy for Lita in Singapore. Her previous job, she told me, had been the complete opposite. It was "like working in hell." Not unlike Albert's employers, Lita's prior boss micromanaged her and ordered her around at all hours. One of her duties had even been to tickle her employers' feet. It supposedly helped them go to sleep. They had Lita do this at all hours of the night, depending on when they returned home in the evening. Sometimes they even woke her up at 2 a.m. While there, she had access to neither a telephone nor the internet, which meant that she could not communicate with her three daughters. Her days off were also sporadic, and when she did have one, her employers would explicitly tell her she could not wear makeup. Before finding her current employer, Lita thought that the conditions in her previous job were standard. She thought it was normal when her agency insisted on confiscating her makeup, jewelry, and mobile phone when she stayed with them while in between jobs. Indeed, this is common practice among agencies in Singapore. They confiscate these items and then present them to employers upon hiring, allowing employers to decide what domestic workers can have in their possession.

It is not unusual for employers to engage in what can be described as the corporal management of domestic workers. Employers can dictate what leisure activities are permittable and even how domestic workers present themselves inside and outside employers' homes, including what workers wear and how they style their hair. In Hong Kong, anthropologist Nicole Constable observed that employers selected clothes and hairstyles for their domestic workers that would make them appear less feminine, so they wouldn't attract the attention of male members of the household. To Lita's surprise, her new employers were different. When the agent handed Lita's makeup to her employers, one responded, "I do not need this. Just give them to her. Those are her personal effects. I have no right to them."

Knowing that there are employers like Lita's gives domestic workers like Albert hope. Like Lita, they tolerate the most intolerable of work situations in hope of eventually securing a job in a household where domestic workers are, in their own words, "not enslaved but free."

Albert's and Lita's experiences speak to the diversity of labor standards for domestic workers across households in Singapore and Dubai. Some workers have a day off and others do not. Some are allowed to do part-time jobs in other households, but most are not. Most receive their salary at the end of each month, but some are not paid until the end of their two-year labor contract. Most have private bedrooms, but some are forced to sleep in hallways or kitchens. Some have access to a mobile phone and internet services, and others do not, preventing them from keeping in touch with family back home. Some are overworked, up to 18 hours a day, while others work for less than 8 hours a day. A few have faced extreme brutality at work. Some women I met at migrant shelters had been raped, tortured, and starved. A consistent theme among these diverse experiences is one of vulnerability. Kafala-like indenture and debt peonage do not universally lead to trafficking, but these systems do put workers at risk of it.

Besides domestic workers, there are other migrant workers who are subjected to a kafala or kafala-like system, though the outcomes are not as consistently negative as for those who perform domestic labor in private houses. These other migrants include the construction workers who built stadiums for the World Cup in Qatar and drywall installers with six-month H-2B visas working seasonally in Phoenix, Arizona; mechanical engineers employed by an oil company in the Kingdom of Saudi Arabia as well as software engineers working with a three-year H-1B visa for a high-tech firm in Redmond, Washington; and finally, nurses under contract in a hospital in Detroit, Michigan, and in Riyadh, Saudi Arabia. It is difficult for any of these workers to quit their job because they are legally bound to their employer.

Indenture for these workers does not necessarily result in forced labor. Consider the hypothetical case of an H-1B visa worker from India employed as a software developer by a firm in Washington state. Many have written about these workers' less-than-ideal work conditions, including long hours and undesirable assignments. Technically someone in their situation has the option to quit and change sponsors, but they would need to get a new H-1B visa, which is all but impossible to do. These visas are allocated via a lottery system, with employer demand usually exceeding the annual cap of 85,000 workers. This means that an employer who wishes to hire a worker and for whom the worker wants to work might not be able to obtain an H-1B visa to legally employ them.

Yet the well-paid software developer is not exactly suffering from forced labor. As described in separate studies by researchers Amy Bhatt and Pallavi Banerjee, these workers enjoy relatively high salaries, guaranteed weekly days off, paid vacations, and potentially even annual bonuses. Unlike domestic laborers, they can freely quit their job and return home. Because they decide to stay in the undesirable job, H-1B visa workers find themselves in a situation we might call *indentured mobility*, that is, as migrant workers who sacrifice their freedom for material gain and the possibility of permanent residency in the United States. When a person makes a decision within the context of severe structural constraints, they enjoy what philosophers such as John Christman call "positive liberty," which describes the freedom of an individual to choose unfreedom.

There are migrant domestic workers, too, whose work conditions are more accurately described as indentured mobility than as forced labor. The former describes those with ideal, task-based work conditions, reasonable hours, regular days off, and higher salaries. Conditions cross into forced labor when the person faces penalties for quitting, operates in undesirable work conditions that they then cannot reject or refuse, and has wages stolen or garnished to pay visa costs. For example, Sanaya, who wants to quit but has been barred from doing so by Irene, suffers from a condition of forced labor.

Irene, of course, does not consider herself a bad person, nor does she think she exploits Sanaya. She would likely be surprised to discover she is engaging in forced labor—much less human trafficking. The last chapter of this book turns to the employer's perspective to try to understand the forces that lead some employers to become "exploiters" and others to be "anti-exploiters."

CHAPTER 3

EXPLOITERS OF FORCED LABOR

—

IRENE CONSIDERS HERSELF a good employer. After all, she allows Sanaya to augment her earnings by cleaning other people's homes. Yet, when she does, Irene collects half of Sanaya's earnings. "I will keep 15 [dirhams; $4] and she'll keep 15," admits Irene. She feels entitled to a portion of Sanaya's earnings because, as Irene explains, she is "still paying her the same salary."

A key distinction between what we might call "exploiters" and "anti-exploiters" comes down to a perception of the employee's time. Time-oriented employers like Irene see their provision of a monthly salary as guaranteeing them control over the labor output of domestic workers for a particular set of hours, which in the United Arab Emirates would be a minimum of 12 hours per day for at least six days each week. Time-oriented employers often expect domestic workers to work continuously and thereby tack on more work once tasks are completed. Time-oriented employers tend to be "exploiters," who maintain a sense of ownership over domestic workers.* To be a time-oriented employer does not mean merely expecting a worker to be available within earmarked periods of a day, let us say nine to five; instead, it is to demand not just continuous but intense labor during this entire period, while reducing the worker's autonomy by determining the pace of completing tasks at hand. To demand nonstop work is inhumane but that is what time-oriented employers expect of domestic workers. Those who find themselves in this situation are those I know to have lost significant weight, with some as much as 15 kilos, more than 30 pounds, within their first six months of employment.

Anti-exploiters have no such sense of ownership and entitlement over the embodied existence of the worker. One of the more mindful employers I met was a schoolteacher named Kat. Kat is one of 240,000 expatriates from Great Britain residing in Dubai. Unlike Irene, Kat sticks to the terms of her live-in domestic worker's contract and avoids adding extra work to the worker's schedule. When she does, Kat is vigilant about recognizing these extra tasks and compensates her worker appropriately. For instance, each time she has the worker babysit in the evening Kat insists on paying her the prevailing wage of 30 dirhams per hour, which is around $8. This is on top of her monthly salary of nearly $600. Though the kafala grants her enormous power over her domestic worker, Kat's task-oriented management style makes her an anti-exploiter. She rigorously avoids forced labor and preserves the worker's autonomy under the terms of

---

* It is not just employers who feel a sense of time ownership. When I lived in Singapore, a friend asked me if the domestic worker I had hired could feed their cat and water their plants while they were away on holiday. My friend did not offer compensation; they assumed it was I doing them the favor. When I asked them to pay her, they changed their mind.

the indenture. Once the worker has completed the assignments Kat has given her, the worker can do as she pleases, whether it is rest, chat on the phone, pursue a hobby, exercise, or work under the table in another household.

Besides the distinction between time-oriented employers and task-oriented ones, there are other attitudes and structures that invite exploitative behaviors, all of which I observed over months of research with domestic laborers and employers in Singapore. It is worth telling one employer's story in detail to uncover the key themes in the exploiter/anti-exploiter dynamic.

IT WAS 2016 AND toward the end of the summer in Singapore. Beatrice, a recent transplant to the city, was not used to the warm humidity. Born and raised in Chicago, Beatrice, who is a second-generation Asian American, came to Singapore by way of Western Europe, where she had been working as a jewelry designer for nearly a decade. Running late to her appointment, she scurried out of a taxi to the foyer of Far East Shopping Plaza hoping to be welcomed by a blast of cool air. But the building, which houses around 600 retail shops, lacks central air-conditioning. Unlike its neighboring structures on famous Orchard Road in the city center, this building does not boast high-end boutiques like Chanel, Louis Vuitton, or Hermès, which have storefronts just across the street. Except for the row of golf shops on the second floor, tailor shops on the first floor, and a few aesthetician studios, most offices in the building are rented by what are known as "maid agencies."

Hundreds of maid agencies operate in Singapore, mostly under license from the Ministry of Manpower. They process the labor and migration of domestic workers from poor neighboring countries such as Indonesia, Myanmar, and Philippines. Maid agencies ensure that prospective domestic workers meet their country of origin's exit requirements, including the completion of skills training, police clearance, and mandatory seminars, as well as the destination country's hiring requirements. In Singapore, these requirements include a medical screening and a test of basic literacy and numeracy skills.

Beatrice found the building unwelcoming, humid and dark, with dim lights and gray flooring. Ironically, the agency that Beatrice was looking for was named Horizons. Unable to locate a building directory, Beatrice was forced to circle each floor, past an endless line of other agencies. The glass doors were illuminated with names like Maidcity, Best Choice Employment Services, A1 Employment Agency, Swift Personnel, and Kensington Maid Manpower Service. Most were small and occupied no more than a closet-sized room that could barely fit a desk and a handful of chairs. Countless women sat against the walls inside and outside each agency. Beatrice soon realized that the women were trying to make eye contact with her. Beatrice politely returned their gazes and even smiled occasionally, but the faces of the women started to blur and she concentrated instead on the door signs, looking for Horizons Agency.

Beatrice is a 33-year-old mother of a 10-month-old. Her husband had been reassigned by his firm from Geneva to Singapore. In Switzerland, they relied on a Latina woman who worked in their home from nine in the morning to six in the evening. In Singapore, Beatrice learned that they could not maintain a similar arrangement because domestic workers are required to reside in their employer's home. This law causes difficulty for some employers, as housing is scarce and expensive in Singapore and few people have extra bedrooms. However, a separate law requires each new flat or house built after 1997 to have a bomb shelter. This space is often a windowless room no bigger than a pantry. Some use it for storage. Others use it to house a domestic worker.

Married to a successful investment banker, Beatrice could well afford to hire a domestic worker. Still, she was surprised at how little it would cost. In Singapore, salaries of domestic workers vary by nationality. Filipinos command salaries starting at S$550, or US$400 per month; those from Indonesia start slightly lower, at S$500 ($375); and those from Myanmar are paid less still: S$450 ($335). A good starting monthly wage would be S$750 ($560). Anything above that would be considered extravagant.

From the signs in front of each agency, Beatrice could see prices as low as S$350 per month to hire a domestic worker from Myanmar. In the United States, this would amount to a mere $260. In Switzerland, she had paid a housekeeper nearly $4,000 each month. The different salary scales of domestic workers, while seemingly discriminatory, are not illegal. They are arbitrarily determined by agencies. Most agency staff I spoke to explained that Filipinos can command a higher salary due to their greater proficiency in English, which is the default lingua franca in Singapore, a former colony of Great Britain. The staff at one agency told me, shockingly, that Indonesians are known to steal and are not as bright as their counterparts from the Philippines, hence the higher wages for Filipinos. The lower rate for domestic workers from Myanmar is explained by their supposed desperation from years of military conflict and ethnic uprisings.

The maid agency services are not free. Employers are charged a fee equivalent to the monthly salary of the domestic worker. The workers themselves are charged much more. Domestic workers from Indonesia are usually expected to pay an equivalent of at least seven months' pay in exchange for securing a minimum of two years of employment in Singapore. Indonesians who are already in Singapore but wish to transfer jobs pay a lesser fee, equivalent to two months of their earnings. Those from the Philippines pay less, either one month's worth of their earnings if transferring jobs within Singapore or at least three months' worth if traveling from the Philippines. Still, I met many from the Philippines who paid as much as their counterparts from Indonesia. Indonesians are said to pay more because they are beholden to not only the Singaporean maid agency but also the Indonesian agency that processes their migration. They remain indebted to the Indonesian agency for as long as they live in Singapore and must pay the agency a fee equivalent to their monthly salary each time they change jobs. In contrast, Filipino domestic workers are bound in debt to the agency in the Philippines only during the initial migration placement.

Horizons was tucked into a corner of the fourth floor. It was Sunday afternoon, the usual day off for domestic workers, and the agency was bustling with activity. Employers walked in and out among dozens of domestic workers who were spending their time off at Horizons in hopes of securing a new position. One of the women in the agency that day was Soraya, a frail and short Indonesian woman who had crossed the border a few days prior from neighboring Batam, and another was Rose, a single mother of three from the Philippines who had recently been terminated and released from her last job. Rose was living at an accommodation provided by the agency for the price of S$15 per day. The others were mostly at the tail end of their two-year employment contract and were hoping to secure a new employer before their visa sponsorship ended.

Unlike most of the other women at Horizons, Rose no longer had a domestic worker visa. Instead, she held a two-week tourist visa. Before her domestic worker visa lapsed, Rose, escorted by a staff member of Horizons, had exited Singapore, crossed the border to Johor Bahru in Malaysia, and then reentered with a tourist visa. She was hoping to secure a 30-day visa but was unfortunately given only 14 days by the immigration officer. This meant that she had only two weeks to find a new employer. Rose did not wish to repeat this trip, as Horizons charges its clients S$300, or US$223, for this border-crossing service. This visa run, which includes a three-night stay at an accommodation, had only added to her debt. The manager at Horizons had Rose's dossier—a 10-page document that includes her passport-sized photo; biodata such as age, height, and weight; medical history; employment history; and letters of recommendation from previous employers—on top of the stack she handed Beatrice.

Beatrice did not expect a lot from a domestic worker; her only requirement was previous experience with childcare. Other tasks, such as cooking and cleaning, were less of a priority for her. She also wanted someone proficient in English, which, according to the manager, limited her selection to Filipinos, who often learn English in school. The stack of dossiers on her lap—all 20 of them—were of workers who met Beatrice's criteria. Beatrice found it difficult to decide. To her, the dossiers all looked the same, the only difference being the picture of the woman on the front page. Yet even the pictures were very similar, as the agency had asked the women to dress in a kind of uniform: white polo shirt with hair pulled back from makeup-free faces. All gave a pursed-lip smile. All had experience with children and all cooked well, with the slight difference being that some had more experience cooking Chinese food than Western cuisine. All boasted glowing reviews from previous employers.

Beatrice was about to ask the manager for more information about the hiring process when they were interrupted by an elderly couple who barged in and announced, "We need to hire maid immediately." Seemingly used to this type of interruption, the manager looked at Beatrice apologetically, then entertained the couple by asking a series of questions: "How many people live in your house?" "How big is your house?" and "Do you give a day off?" The couple avoided the last question, responding, "We need flexibility because we throw many parties." The manager proceeded to tell them that she did not think there was anyone available for them to hire but they could leave their phone number in case something changed. In response to the surprised look on Beatrice's face, the manager explained that she could already see that this employer would be very strict, difficult, and unlikely to grant a day off. She suspected these employers were the type who quickly cycle through domestic workers.

This manager admitted to dismissing many employers. She refuses to work with anyone who imposes what she perceives to be less than fair standards. She accordingly gauges each prospective employer as they walk into the agency, immediately asking about their policy for a day off, the size of their house and household, their diet, their labor expectations such as frequency of cleaning, ironing, and cooking, and so forth. Based on the responses, she then refuses those who admit to denying a day off, paying a low salary, or having excessively high work demands. An employer with too many pets, such as the employer with 20 birds, would be denied their business.

While the agency earns fees each time an employer wants a new employee, there are risks to catering to difficult employers. The

Singapore government monitors the domestic worker market and looks suspiciously at employers and agencies guilty of frequent turnovers. The government has outsourced the processing of domestic employment to agencies since it formalized its reliance on migrant workers under the 1978 Foreign Maid Scheme. Preceding this was the Employment Agencies Act of 1958. Despite its reliance on the market, the state monitors foreign-employee placement closely, including domestic work.

Toward this effort, the state implemented the Employers' Orientation Programme, which is a three-hour course on an employer's roles and responsibilities in managing a foreign domestic worker. The course is required of all first-time employers, who must also complete an exam with a passing rate of 80 percent. The course and the exam put a lot of emphasis on food and work safety, teaching employers basic nutrition, such as the maximum number of eggs that domestic workers should consume in a week, and safety practices such as the proper use of a ladder. Employers who are quick to fire domestic workers sometimes face state discipline, including having to retake the mandatory supervisory class or being temporarily barred from hiring a domestic worker. Agencies could also risk losing their business license. This is why they tend to avoid "fussy" employers—and there seemed to be many at Horizons.

Not long after the elderly couple left, another client noisily entered the agency. The employer, a petite woman close to Beatrice in age, strode into the room while a much smaller woman meekly walked behind her lugging a tiny duffle bag and a carry-on suitcase. The woman announced, "I am returning this domestic worker. She give me too many problems with food." The manager again diverted her attention from Beatrice. The employer complained that her domestic worker ate too much. This surprised Beatrice. The domestic worker looked quite small, even frail, and did not have the appearance of someone who overeats. Yet this employer insisted that she did. The employer said that she was not starving her domestic worker; she explained that she fed the worker an apple and a glass of milk each morning. The problem, she said, was that this worker always chose the largest apple. Then, as if to gain the sympathy of others in the room, including Beatrice, the employer complained about the time the domestic worker had eaten half of a tofu package instead of the quarter she was instructed to eat for dinner one evening.

For Beatrice, it was difficult to believe that employers would limit the food consumed by domestic workers. Yet here was an employer firing a domestic worker for this very reason. Beatrice then began to wonder how the manager was going to mediate this conflict. Was she going to reprimand the domestic worker? Or was she going to find a way to criticize the employer? As if reading Beatrice's mind, the manager turned to the domestic worker, who Beatrice learned was named Jonna, and asked if she wanted to be "exchanged" to another household. She did. This seemed to resolve the conflict. The manager then turned to the employer, apologized about the mismatched placement, and arranged to have them return midweek to start the process of looking for a replacement hire. The employer then stood up and walked out the door without even saying goodbye to Jonna, who did not seem at all heartbroken about being fired. And even though she had just incurred enormous expenses, a one-month wage penalty for early termination and one month's worth of her wages for the job-placement fee, Jonna seemed relieved. As she explained to the manager and everyone else in the small room, this employer had been unbearable, demanding long hours, depriving her of adequate food, and limiting her to only one day off each month.

Beatrice could see how both the elderly couple and the young mother were likely to be undesirable employers. Yet she still could not help but wonder why the agency staff would not recommend Rose or Soraya, two people who were clearly in need of a job and would likely welcome any employment opportunity. The longer they could not find work, the bigger their debt to the agency. Beatrice asked the manager about this, but she got her answer from the dozens of women seated nearby, who muttered phrases like "difficult employer," "too hard," and "strict." In the case of the elderly couple, the women around Beatrice explained that having to clean a three-story house plus cater to the whims of the family, which consisted of five adults, would be too taxing and laborious. All agreed that it would be much better to risk the wait for a less demanding employer. Yes, they might accrue debt now, but if they agreed to be placed in the household of a "fussy" employer, they would likely be fired and charged the wage penalties, which might potentially be much higher.

With the interruptions over, Beatrice turned back to the dossiers. Beatrice found the biodata to be particularly curious; they included the age, height, weight, and even skin-tone choices of tan, dark, or light for domestic workers. Physical features matter because, according to the manager of Horizons, they determine the ability of domestic workers to do their required tasks. For instance, those whose house has tall windows will likely wish to hire a domestic worker "more than five feet tall." Anthropologist Nicole Constable has likewise observed the use of physical features by employers when deciding on domestic workers in Hong Kong. The face matters, for instance, because employers often don't want to hire someone too attractive or someone whose features would be considered unlucky in feng shui, a traditional Chinese practice that uses energy to harmonize individuals with their environment. Asked later what it was like to hire a domestic worker in Singapore, Beatrice described it as a "bizarre meat market" that "feels a little bit like people-trading."

Feeling overwhelmed, Beatrice ultimately asked the manager of Horizons to select a domestic worker for her. The manager politely declined. Instead, she asked Beatrice to join her at the back of the room, away from the domestic workers in the office. She then proceeded to go through a process of elimination, identifying potential problems with each one of the applicants. She first eliminated the ones with boyfriends: They could be tempted to bring unwanted guests over. Then she dismissed those whose skills were not as good as they seemed on paper, such as the less skilled cooks. Beatrice was eventually left with five potential hires, including Rose.

After helping Beatrice narrow her selection, the manager looked up to see if the five potential hires were still around the agency. The manager then called out each of their names to inform them that they were going to be interviewed by Beatrice. The five were pleased, as working for an expatriate from Europe or North America is a coveted job that is thought to pay more, offer more consistent days off, and provide adequate food, rest, and privacy. Beatrice still struggled to make a choice. The answers they all gave to her questions, most of which concerned their experience with babies, seemed the same. With the prodding of agency staff, Beatrice ultimately decided on Rose. When she learned she had won the job, Rose beamed. She was finally going to be able to pay off her debt.

The manager then began to mediate the terms of employment by asking Beatrice what seemed to be an endless number of questions:

What time should Rose wake up and go to bed, would she have a break in the afternoon, would she have to prepare all or only some of the meals, would she have a food allowance, would she have to do the ironing daily or biweekly, and would she have to clean the house during certain times of the day? Beatrice did not have an answer to any of these questions. Since domestic work is informal work, it is generally advisable for employers and domestic workers to lay out what are agreeable terms of employment before the job begins. But Beatrice thought she was hiring an experienced worker and had not expected she would be asked to micromanage Rose to such an extent.

Beatrice also struggled with how the agency decided on Rose's salary. The dossier of every worker had listed their preferred salary. Rose was asking for S$750 per month, nearly 50 percent higher than the average starting salary of S$550 for domestic workers from the Philippines, yet commensurate with Rose's seven years of experience in Singapore. Beatrice thought this to be a fair request, but the manager disagreed and initiated the salary negotiation, stating that Rose's request was too high, instead recommending a salary of S$650. Beatrice sat quietly, unsure whether she should argue with the manager, but before she could say anything Rose conceded to the lesser amount. The manager then added that if Rose performed well after six months, then maybe Beatrice would be willing to give her a raise.

Beatrice had not done much to vet Horizons as an agency. Her neighbor, a schoolteacher from Australia, had recommended the agency, saying that she had chosen Horizons because it did not impose high fees or recommend oppressive labor standards for domestic workers. Agencies see their work as helping employers and domestic workers find a happy medium: calling out employers when they expect too much, letting them know if they expect too little, and guiding those who come in without any expectations at all. Beatrice would fall into the last group, which is why the manager felt comfortable determining Rose's salary and advising Beatrice to design a schedule, one that included set rest periods. Indeed, Horizons is more principled than many agencies. They do not advise employers to monitor the phone calls of domestic workers, restrict their access to the internet, or hold their passports. In other words, they do not condone restricting the freedom of domestic workers. Some agencies I visited did.

Instead, the manager at Horizons knew to ask key questions to set certain employer expectations: Would Beatrice give Rose a day off? How often? It wasn't until 2013 that Singapore granted domestic workers the right to a weekly day off. This was a legislative change prompted by the passage of the 2011 ILO Convention on Decent Work for Domestic Workers. While many employers now grant their domestic workers a weekly day off, not all do. Some employers opt instead to buy their workers out of their days off. Domestic workers receive the equivalent of their daily wage rate calculated from their monthly salary. As one employer, a young manager at a beauty salon, explained, "It's her [monthly] salary of $450 divided by 26 so per day is like $18." In U.S. dollars, this would be compensating someone $13.50 for a day's work. As of 2023, the government has mandated the provision of at least one day off per month, preventing employers from buying out all their employee's weekly days off.

The manager at Horizons continued with her questions. Would Beatrice hold the worker's passport? Would they have access to a cellular phone? These questions caught Beatrice by surprise, but the manager at Horizons explained that employers in Singapore determine the degree of domestic workers' freedoms. Some employers insist on holding a worker's passport to deter them from running away, while others do so for the employee's "safekeeping." Beatrice would do neither.

Beatrice soon had another moral dilemma to confront: how to settle Rose's debts. Rose had accrued charges from the agency for crossing the border to Malaysia for a new visa, staying at the agency's residence, and using its job placement services. If Beatrice wished to hire Rose, or—as the manager informed her—any domestic worker in Singapore, for that matter, Beatrice would be obligated to loan Rose money up front to cover that debt. Rose would then repay this debt through a peonage system. Beatrice would deduct most if not all of Rose's salary until the debt was paid in full.

Rose's debt amounted to nearly S$2,000. According to the manager, Rose's new salary of S$650 would cover the debt in three months. As a "transfer maid," meaning someone changing jobs in Singapore, Rose's debt was lower than that of a newcomer. For instance, Soraya, the frail woman who had just arrived from Indonesia, entered Singapore saddled with a debt worth eight months of her salary. In both cases, the dollar figure of the debt seemed arbitrary. If Soraya were to earn a starting salary of S$450 per month, then a prospective employer would have to fork over at least S$3,600 to the agency. If she were to earn S$350, then this amount would be S$2,800. Regardless of the amount, the common understanding was that Soraya would not receive a salary for her first eight months of employment.

No one knows why agency fees are calculated by time and not money, yet in almost every country I have studied, debts are calculated this way. The only exception is Canada, where agencies charge the domestic worker an up-front fee, which could be as low as $5,500 or as high as $10,000 for a temporary work visa and guaranteed job placement in a private household that will pay them at least 3,000 Canadian dollars per month. The fees charged by agencies vary across countries, with higher-paying destinations such as Canada charging more. The up-front payment expected in Canada makes the country inaccessible for most domestic workers. Different types of "fly now, pay later" schema make other destinations accessible, as do loans. In both Hong Kong and Taiwan, domestic workers borrow from lending agencies. In Singapore, domestic workers borrow from employers.

Reviewing the newly drafted contract, Beatrice saw that she was obligated to give Rose a monthly allowance of only S$10 during her first three months in the job. Asked to justify this small amount, the manager explained to Beatrice that this was more of a gift that the domestic worker can use to purchase phone cards to speak to their children back home. Beatrice was not comfortable with this arrangement, and she let the agency staff know this. But the manager reassured her that Rose should be able to manage adequately even without a salary because Beatrice would be providing her with food and shelter. She then advised Beatrice to help Rose keep her expenses low during this time by denying her a day off until her debt was paid in full. The manager said this was a common practice when dealing with domestic workers bound in debt.

Beatrice understood that this form of peonage was ubiquitous in Singapore, but she refused to participate in it. Beatrice decided to ignore the terms of the contract, forgive Rose's debt, and immediately begin paying her a salary at the end of her first month of employment. Beatrice also decided to pay Rose more than their agreed amount of S$650 by giving her a monthly allowance of S$100 for additional food and incidentals.

Beatrice is a rarity among employers. Many just follow the recommendations of maid agencies and subject their household workers to peonage. It is easy to just blindly follow what one is told is common practice. I experienced this myself in the summer of 2016, when my husband, Ben, and I temporarily relocated to Southeast Asia and went through the process of hiring a domestic worker in Singapore.

Ben and I could not afford to hire a live-in domestic worker in the United States, where salary alone would be more than $2,500 per month, plus Social Security contributions, food, and accommodations. In contrast, even with the added cost of food, medical insurance, and the government levy of S$300 per month, the price of domestic help in Singapore was within our budget.

We needed a domestic worker for only six months. Ironically, this made it a challenge to find one. Most domestic workers want at least a two-year labor contract in exchange for the hefty fee imposed by agencies. This left my husband and me to choose from a small pool of the most desperate people: those needing a new visa sponsor and facing deportation, those awaiting new positions and accumulating debt, and those seeking to escape intolerable work conditions. Being Filipino American myself did not help; Filipino employers have the worst reputation among domestic workers, who assume them to be *matapobre*, meaning someone who looks down on the poor. Historian Filomeno Aguilar Jr. has observed class tensions between skilled and unskilled workers in the Filipino diaspora, with the skilled troubled by their frequent misidentification as unskilled workers. Skilled workers have reacted by distancing themselves from the "poor," including domestic workers. Filipino employers are also assumed to be more likely than others to impose an employer savior complex and pay a paltry salary more fitting of what someone would earn in the Philippines. It took some convincing from agency staff before workers would consider working for me, despite our shared ethnicity. We ended up hiring a woman named Ria.

Ria was a victim of human trafficking. Her previous employers had duped her. They said she would be working for a single family, but instead she had to care for a household of 14 adults: cooking meals, packing lunches, ironing clothes, washing towels and bedsheets, and doing anything else they might require. Ria had started this job with a debt equivalent to seven months of her salary, which she still had not fully paid by the time she quit to work in my household. Not only had Ria done more work than she had been expecting, but she had also not been paid for six months of labor.

Quitting should have been easy for her. The Singapore Prevention of Human Trafficking Act of 2014 grants victims the right to temporary shelter and counseling services if they approach the Ministry of Manpower. Yet Ria did not know that her experience qualified her for support. Instead, she returned to her agency, where she was penalized for failing to complete her labor contract and charged a one-month wage penalty.

Hiring Ria ultimately cost us S$3,000. This amount, we were told, included Ria's debt of S$1,950, or three months of work. The agency told us that withholding her wages to repay this debt was standard procedure. Like Beatrice, we were advised to limit her days off to minimize her expenses. In the United States, this is illegal, but not in Singapore. As soon as we walked out, I looked at my husband and told him, "We are not going to confiscate Ria's wages." My husband agreed—the costs would be a much smaller burden to us than they would be to her—but he admitted that he had not realized what was going on and likely would have followed the agency's instructions if not for me.

The debt accrued by migrant domestic workers to secure a job puts them at risk of human trafficking. This raises the question of why employers go along with it. Some employers see no wrongdoing at all. Others sense that something is off about the transaction and will quickly tell you they do not condone peonage or other exploitative practices, and yet they go along with it to avoid any awkwardness with agency staff. Others comply for purely practical purposes. Some employers, like Beatrice and myself, absorb the domestic worker's debt. I would like to think of myself as an anti-exploiter, someone who consciously rejected the system of debt bondage in Singapore and thereby minimized my risk of becoming a trafficker. But my actions admittedly did nothing to change the larger maid agency system. The most I could do was offer Ria the option to extricate herself from debt bondage, which I did initially by paying off her debt and then later by offering to pay for her next set of agency fees once she left my employment. Most Filipino domestic workers aim to return home and start a business that will generate a profit sufficient to sustain them in the Philippines. Ben and I also offered Ria the capital to do just that. She took us up on this offer and accepted our gift of S$3,000, which allowed her to open a small-scale *babuyan*, or piggery, in her hometown.

Based on my research among employers in Singapore and Dubai, I have identified a number of key ideas that explain why employers victimize their workers and engage in a peonage system, as well as how they justify their complicity in such a system. One set of dynamics is rooted in capitalism and the market and is best exemplified by what I witnessed in Singapore. Another operates within the complex social structures of race and nationality and is best exemplified by dynamics I observed in Dubai. We'll go to Dubai first.

"Forced labor" elicits assumptions of horrific violence. Yet most crimes of forced labor can seem mundane: assigning an extra task, asking an employee to work longer hours, or forcing them to work on their day off. Most forced-labor exploiters do not coercively extract labor by brute force, but this does not mean that extreme abuse does not happen. Take the case of Irene, the Oregonian in Dubai, who refused to release her employee, Sanaya, from her contract to seek new employment.

While employers can include sadistic people who take pleasure in inflicting cruelty on others, most victimizers do not consciously harm domestic workers. Time-oriented employers like Irene unwittingly exploit workers because they do not see anything wrong when they change their plans at the last minute, resulting in a lost day off. Many even consider themselves good employers. As Irene said, "We're very lenient. We're very relaxed. We give her a lot of freedom."

While it is easy to blame class or culture, neither one can fully explain employers' bad behavior. Employers with less means are not necessarily more likely to abuse domestic workers. There is also no specific ethnic group we can accuse and typecast as more likely to harm and overwork domestic workers. To help explain why employers take advantage of their power, it helps to consider a concept called "pernicious ignorance." A term coined by Black feminist philosopher Kristie Dotson, pernicious ignorance in this case refers to the ways employers see domestic employment solely from their own perspective and are blind to the epistemic harm they inflict on workers. An example of pernicious ignorance is Irene focusing on the money she would lose if she let Sanaya quit, instead of on the ways in which Sanaya herself is entrapped.

Racism often fuels pernicious ignorance for Irene and other Western expatriates in Dubai. In this case, it's not racism against their African or Asian domestic worker but rather racism against their Arab neighbors. There are many Western expatriates who insist that their treatment of domestic workers can never be as bad as that of the Arabs around them. Considering themselves superior to their neighbors allows employers like Irene to avoid recognizing their own bad behavior. I call this practice racist self-deflection, and it is a key driver of exploitation by Western employers in Dubai.

To deflect from the way she exploits Sanaya, Irene often complains about her Khaleeji neighbors from Kuwait. According to Irene, it is in their nature to oppress domestic workers. She says they even encourage their children to abuse the employee. In the interview, she leaned forward to underscore her disapproval and said: "They have a housekeeper. They have a driver. They have a nanny. And the kids are monsters. Because they learn that they can treat them in a certain way and get away with it. . . . The housekeeper and the nanny are so afraid of losing their job, they let the kids do whatever they want. They treat them so poorly." In contrast, Irene thinks of herself as a staunch advocate of human rights. One day she even confronted her neighbors about the way they mistreat their domestic workers, who Irene says are paid as little as $220 a month and denied a day off. Irene recounts their conversation: "I said, 'How could you not let her leave? . . . How does she get exercise?'" According to Irene, the neighbor responded, "She can run around the house if she wants." Irene thinks it is inhumane for her neighbors to bar their domestic workers from leaving the house. This imposed isolation, she says, puts the mental health of domestic workers at risk. Irene complains that her neighbor thinks that her domestic worker doesn't need friends because "she has us." She says this mistreatment occurs widely among "Arabs who have been used to housekeepers their whole lives." As she states, "When it comes to housekeepers, this is how it is." Regardless of how her Khaleeji neighbors treat their domestic workers, Irene's criticism blinds her to her own faults as an employer.

As a white woman, Irene distances herself from her Khaleeji neighbors, aligning herself with other Western expatriates from "Australia, South Africa, all over Europe, America, Canada, and even South America." As a group, she asserts, Westerners treat domestic workers better and "pay fair wages" compared to their Arab neighbors. Yet Irene herself pays Sanaya a below-average salary and is inconsistent in her provision of a day off. Still, Irene brags about her supposed superior treatment of Sanaya and other domestic workers she has employed, insisting, "We pay more than the minimum. And we treat our employees well. Westerners—they are nicer. Because they will pay more. Because they will give them more leniency than the Arabs."

Irene's sentiments concerning her Arab neighbors are shared by other Western employers in Dubai. Matt, a British finance manager, observed, "You'll find a big difference in the way maids are treated depending on the nationality of the employer. So, what we have heard is that those who are employed by locals [Emiratis] and by GCC [Gulf Cooperation Countries] employers like those from Saudi and places like that, are treated far worse than we, the Western expats, treat their maids."

Matt considers himself a good employer because he pays his

domestic worker an above-average salary and rewards her regularly with bonuses. He also says that he makes sure to grant her a weekly day off. Yet he soon admitted that he regularly requires his employee to work more than 18 hours a day. Matt confessed that he doesn't think much about his domestic worker's schedule. He requires her to always be available when he needs her. In his household, he expects the domestic worker to stay up if someone in his family is awake. This means that the domestic worker regularly finds herself having to be up until 2 a.m. even if she must be up by 6. On top of this, and in contrast to his earlier assertion about being consistent with days off, Matt admitted that he regularly spoils her weekend plans, canceling her day off at the last minute to accommodate his own social needs. Matt does not seem to have any qualms about inconveniencing his domestic worker. Supposedly neither does she. According to him, she never complains or shows resentment. Instead, she meekly acquiesces to his demands by saying, "Oh, oh, no problem, Sir. It doesn't matter," or, "I'll meet my friends tomorrow." She likely feels powerless to respond any differently.

Racist self-deflection allows employers like Irene and Matt to genuinely believe that their worst treatment of domestic workers will always be better than the labor conditions imposed by their Arab neighbors, and their beliefs do not emerge from a vacuum. Their behavior fits what Palestinian literary critic Edward Said calls "Orientalism," meaning prejudiced interpretations of the Orient, particularly the Arab World, and the view of their cultural practices as backward. Often spread through popular culture, Orientalism presumes Western superiority through negative images of the Orient that exaggerate differences between the Orient and the Occident. The Orient, depicted as a place of barbarism, is where domestic workers confront the brutal treatment of employers. Though they benefit from the "Orientalist" system of the kafala, Western employers like Irene and Matt place themselves outside this system and consider themselves exempt from committing the abuse that this system invites. This logic allows them to impose abysmal work conditions, including extensive hours and low pay, while denying their ill treatment of domestic workers.

Another key component of racist self-deflection, and an overall Orientalist attitude, is the employer savior complex. As discussed earlier, many employers feel justified in offering subpar working conditions because even those subpar conditions are better than what their employee might have experienced had they not become a migrant worker. Both Matt and Irene are convinced that their workers' current lives are significantly better than the lives they would have had in their home countries—and better, too, than what they'd experience if they worked for the Kuwaiti employer next door. This logic allows both Irene and Matt to downplay the harsh standards they may impose. As Irene notes, "If it was really that bad, then they wouldn't be here." Working in Dubai, according to Irene, had been Sanaya's most viable means of escaping the "slums" where she had "nothing." In Dubai, she supposedly "works hard but makes a decent salary." Irene genuinely believes that her employment rescued Sanaya from a "really very, very bad place."

WESTERN EMPLOYERS IN DUBAI, like Matt and Irene, often use racist self-deflection or Orientalist thinking to justify exploitative behavior. In contrast, employers in Singapore use market-focused and society-based reasons to excuse their behavior. Over a period of 12 months in Singapore, my research assistants and I conducted interviews with more than 30 employers, each of whom held a variety of beliefs that allowed them to deflect guilt for exploiting laborers through the Singaporean peonage system.

A large number of employers (most employers, in fact) simply blamed maid agencies for the debt bondage of domestic workers. One employer, a newlywed named Sushil, was looking to hire a domestic worker for the first time. According to Sushil, employers saddle domestic workers with the brunt of agency fees simply because the employers cannot afford to take on this expense. As he bluntly stated, "If the employer [has to pay] the agency fee, nobody will hire the maid." This does not mean that employers lack sympathy for domestic workers. Many feel sorry for them. As one laments: "They get no money for six months. The agency takes all the money. I feel bad for the maid but what can I do? It's 3,000 plus that they have to pay back to agency. I don't want to give to agency. Agencies are evil and unreasonable."

It is true that agencies' policies may seem draconian and exploitative. They charge migrants very high fees and burden them with debt. They flood the market with migrant laborers, putting pressure on the wages workers can command and the conditions of work they must endure. Agencies argue that in exchange for their fees, they provide migrants access to jobs and income they previously could not access.

Even those employers who suggest that agencies are exploitative and overcharge migrants do concede that the agencies perform valuable labor for employers. As the newlywed Sushil acknowledges: "Well I suppose they are providing a service . . . because they are helping us to select and screen the maid . . . to fit our requirements."

Agencies not only help in hiring and handling Singapore's bureaucratic maze of requirements (as well as those imposed by the worker's country of origin), they also handle the initial management of domestic workers. For example, Nelly, a managing director of a human resource firm, is too busy to train her domestic worker. She depends on the agency for that. As she admitted, "When they first come, first week they all cry. The agency usually comes to my house to lecture them."

Despite providing beneficial services to employers, the cost burdens associated with agencies fall almost entirely on the migrants. Migrants must repay a hefty debt while employers' major up-front costs are returned to them via hundreds of hours of unpaid labor. The saturated market of "maid agencies" means that prospective employers can easily take their business elsewhere, forcing agencies to keep costs to employers low. As one employer observed, "Actually, in a way, it's no cost to the employer because they are actually getting a six-month or so payment from the maid."

All of this offers employers a scapegoat: Employers often claim that the agencies are the true driver of exploitation. But I would argue that since employers benefit greatly from the agencies' services and the peonage system, they are every bit as responsible for its inequalities and abuses and are thus complicit in forced labor.

Employers justify this complicity with deflections. One popular deflection involves suggesting that they've done the worker a favor by paying off their debts up front, and that it is only right that the worker "repay" those debts. In this version of the employer savior complex, employers see the provision of a job as a gift to the domestic worker.

Another popular deflection is to blame the market realities. One employer I talked to, a small-business owner named Melinda, insisted that peonage is nothing but a fair market exchange in which employers have to prepay S$3,000 for someone's labor that they then recoup by having the person "work minimum six months without salary." She quickly attempted to clarify that this did not mean the worker is "without salary" because employers "pay their salary to the agent in advance. And they end up working for no salary for six months, six months to eight months." Employers like Melinda acknowledge that domestic workers pay a steeper agency fee than employers but accept it as nothing but a market reality. As she says, "I find that maid agency fee is very high, but we have no choice because it is the market price. We have no choice. We have to follow."

Melinda's argument suggests that because a "market price" has been reached, the price is both fair and efficient. But in this case the price is not a market reality but rather a "fictitious commodity." As defined by the social theorist Karl Polanyi, a fictitious commodity refers to anything that is commodified, in this case knowledge—specifically the knowledge of locating, vetting, and then hiring a domestic worker—that was not necessarily created for the market. The sharing of this knowledge doesn't have to be a commodity; it could also occur informally through social networks. In its commodification, fees become an arbitrary construction that fuels the exploitation of desperate workers from overseas. As one labor broker put it, "I employ very, very poor people. Look at this woman [pointing to an unemployed domestic worker], she's 51 years old. She do not want to go back. I'm trying to get her employer. She told me if [she] goes back, [she] won't be able to come back to Singapore."

The "market reality" argument focuses on the migrant worker's own agency. These employers feel they should not be blamed for debt bondage when the domestic worker, as a rational actor, *freely chose* to enter an exploitative contract of unfreedom. This logic abides by the notion of "positive liberty" and recognizes the agency of a domestic worker to choose the illiberal position of being bound in debt bondage. Yet often these same employers perpetuate their power in the peonage system by selectively infantilizing the employee, limiting their freedom, such as denying them a day off in order to expedite the payment of debt, via the logic that doing so is for the domestic worker's own good.

Besides blaming the agencies and market reality, employers in Singapore—as in Dubai—often rely on pernicious ignorance to justify the exploitation they perpetrate. They refuse to acknowledge the true meaning of the debt imposed by the agency, and how the resulting peonage fosters vulnerability for the worker and empowers the employer. Historian Robert Proctor, an expert in the study of ignorance, or what he calls agnotology, would argue that employers benefit from their use of "ignorance as strategic ploy."

An important aspect of this ignorance is bureaucratic. The idea of obtaining the proper paperwork for the migrant's visa seems daunting to many employers. Newlywed Sushil expressed his bewilderment at the bureaucracy of migrant domestic work: "But also what is it that they need? Work permit and stuff like that. When you have to apply for the work permit and some of the other documentations, all that right? If you try and do it yourself, it's very, very, very difficult because you have to go through like the Philippines embassy. It's just crazy." Going along with agency recommendations, including peonage, because the paperwork seems too difficult to handle yourself, is another form of deflection.

Perhaps the most dangerous deflection of all, however, is a social one. In this case, employers deny wrongdoing by pointing out that everyone else is doing it, so there must be nothing wrong with it. In this situation, domestic employers justify their complicity in peonage by substituting their personal morals for the prevailing norms.

All these justifications come into play in the case of Amanda, an American transplant to Singapore who sees nothing wrong with subjecting her domestic worker to peonage. An American in her 30s, Amanda is a stay-at-home mother of two young children who, with her husband, a financial analyst, moved to Singapore from Los Angeles. Distinctively tall and slim, she came to the interview dressed casually in a button-down shirt tucked inside loose cropped jeans. Her jewelry, including a pair of one-carat diamond stud earrings, sparkled noticeably. Amanda thinks she is more than just a decent person; she imagines herself to be someone who cares deeply about the well-being of domestic workers.

She volunteers at a migrant worker center, and as a way of demonstrating her care, Amanda always makes sure her domestic worker has "enough food" and "enough vegetables" for every meal. Amanda is health conscious in a very Los Angeles kind of way, which is a value she wishes to extend to her domestic worker. As she shared, "I try to teach her about nutrition, about diet, about health, about, you know, if you have these conditions, so your family has this history, you must not eat this, eat that." Amanda also genuinely worries about the long-term security of her domestic worker. For instance, Amanda is concerned about her domestic worker's lack of savings: "She doesn't have a bank account. That's what I am a bit worried about. So, I don't know what she does with her money. I mean I'd like her to put it into the bank account, but she doesn't seem to want to or she wasn't that set on it, so I didn't force her to. But I do want her to save money for herself."

Despite her good intentions, Amanda could, by some definitions, be labeled a human trafficker. First, her apartment functions as a space of confinement for her domestic worker; Amanda limits her worker to two days off a month. Second, she chooses to hold on to her employee's passport. Third, Amanda pays the worker a salary of merely S$470 per month, or US$360, far below what other expatriates compensate their domestic workers. Finally, she had no qualms subjecting her domestic worker to seven months of peonage in which she paid the worker just S$10 per month. Amanda would likely be mortified to be called a human trafficker, and yet she disregards her domestic worker's underpayment and isolation, her inability to quit her job, and the immorality of debt-based peonage.

Why did Amanda impose such stringent labor conditions? According to her, it's what the maid agency advised. It is curious that Amanda decided to blindly follow their advice. It is not as if Amanda has never hired a domestic worker before. She had employed household help while in Los Angeles, though she had never hired a live-in worker. This inexperience, she explained, made her unsure how to determine the parameters of employment. As she explained, "When we were hiring, we just listened to whatever the agent said. Looking back now based on what my helper told me, I think the starting salary then was $500 a month. But we hired her at $470, which I didn't know was below the salary rate because the agent had suggested that salary. So, we just went with that." Interestingly, the realization that she was paying her domestic worker a salary that was below market rate did not prompt Amanda to increase her worker's pay.

Social pressures also explain why Amanda felt comfortable following the advice of the agency to hold on to the worker's passport. When asked why she chose to keep the passport, she responded, "That is what everyone said to do. The agent gave it to us and told us to keep it." She feels it is important, on some level, to hold the passport because doing so protects the worker from quitting prematurely and thus falling deeper into debt.

How does Amanda justify these abysmal work conditions in her own home? How does she resolve the contradiction between the person she imagines herself to be when she volunteers at a migrant worker center and the employer she actually is? A complex set of social pressures and other deflections come into play. First, Amanda claims to play by the rules, doing what she understands to be socially acceptable. In this case, that means blindly agreeing to the agency's terms, even when she realizes they are subpar. At the same time, she refuses to acknowledge the potential harms she is inflicting from her subpar labor conditions. Amanda sees her domestic worker as both an adult who chose to enter an exploitative contract and an infantilized figure who needs someone to hold her passport for her, structure her diet, manage her financial affairs, and plan her time off.

Amanda also chose to remain ignorant about the terms of peonage, specifically the different amounts charged to her and to her domestic worker. While Amanda paid the agency less than S$1,000, her domestic worker paid nearly S$3,000. When asked why she refused to defray the employee's costs, she explained, "I wasn't going to pay it, because we didn't know what it was for. . . . Even till this day we don't know what it was for, but [the domestic worker] just paid it." Amanda uses this ignorance of the debt to deny accountability. In her mind, the domestic worker had done *something* to incur the debt, so the onus of the debt should not be on her as an employer but on the domestic worker.

Overriding every deflection is the employer savior complex. Deep down, Amanda believes that the lives of domestic workers in Singapore can only be an improvement on their lives prior to migration. In her mind, the harms imposed by peonage cannot outweigh its rewards. Sacrificing one's salary for seven months is better than not having a salary at all. Likewise, a low salary is a vast improvement over whatever salary they had before.

Amanda is not alone in thinking this way. Several employers I spoke to reasoned that sleeping in a hallway was much better than sleeping without a roof over one's head. Again and again, employers made themselves feel better about their poor treatment of domestic workers by insisting that migration had improved those workers' lives. And as employers, they see themselves as the ones responsible for this improvement.

Mark, a real estate manager, pays his domestic worker S$500 a month, denies her a day off, and holds on to her passport. Yet he thinks he is an overall good employer, someone who is considerate of his domestic worker's need to reach out to her family in Indonesia, rest, and eat adequately. Occasionally he even brings her home dinner from McDonald's, which Mark insists is a magnanimous gesture. As he relayed, "She was so happy because McDonald's to her is a luxury, and it was something that she could only afford to do once a year." According to Mark, we should see his domestic worker's labor conditions relatively and realize that whatever he gives her, from the salary to the accommodations, "is really luxurious compared to where she came from."

This employer savior complex—and all the other deflections discussed earlier—allows employers like Mark and Amanda to justify conditions of peonage and the overall subpar labor conditions of their domestic workers. When questioned about the salary-deduction system, employers often react as if they had just been reminded of it. Mark responded by saying, "Wage deduction, yes, I think there was wage deduction for six months. That was from the agency." One after the other, employers would admit being complicit to peonage. Another employer, Melissa, a beauty-supply clerk, shared, "So up front will be 3,000 to 4,000 and the maid will not get any salary for like up to eight months. For every month, we just pay her some allowance like $20." In their matter-of-fact description of the salary-deduction system, what employers ignore is how this experience is excruciating for domestic workers. Vilma, a domestic worker, shared, "It is terribly exhausting to work only not to receive a single cent at the end of the month."

In an environment full of market, racial, and social structures that lead to exploitation, employers must be vigilant if they want to be anti-exploiters. The conclusion of the book will look at some ways individuals can become anti-traffickers and the role global institutions might play in alleviating the problem on a structural level.

CONCLUSION

HOW TO FIGHT FORCED LABOR

Forced labor, the extraction of labor from a person under the menace of penalty, is a global problem. In most countries, it is considered a crime. In the United States, we use powerful language to describe it: peonage, slavery, and human trafficking. The United Nations views forced labor as an urgent crime against humanity in the twenty-first century. Yet it persists.

"Forced labor," "trafficking," and "slavery" are terms I use throughout the book, but not interchangeably. They are forms of subjugation that have similar but slightly different meanings that victims often confront simultaneously. A trafficked person is someone likely also subjected to forced labor (and, in the worst-case scenario, enslavement). Take the case of Pulido. She was trafficked: She was deceived about the circumstances of her relocation to the United States and exploited by being denied a wage. She wanted to return home to the Philippines but couldn't, making her a victim of forced labor. She was also arguably enslaved, as she confronted natal alienation, violence, and the erasure of dignity.

These forms of subjugation—in particular, trafficking and forced labor—loom over domestic work. It is because the conditions of employment invite it: the indenture of migrant domestic workers across the world, including in the United States, United Arab Emirates, and Singapore; the market system that legalizes peonage, as we see in Singapore; and the high costs imposed by migrant agencies, including au pair agencies in the United States. It is a crime often unwittingly perpetrated by domestic employers, many of whom consider themselves genuinely good, moral people. They believe they are treating their workers humanely, despite inadequately feeding or paying them. A modern-day slaveholder like Alex Tizon can genuinely feel akin to a savior. Someone who steals a domestic worker's earnings for work done outside their home can think of themselves as a "good employer." Then there are employers who willfully subject their domestic worker to debt bondage because it is common practice, refusing to confront the moral or ethical problems it raises. Why are these employers blind to their role in human trafficking and forced labor?

While employers have various ways of deflecting blame for their crimes, their behavior can be fully understood only within the context of their social setting. Structural conditions allow employers to subjugate domestic workers. The conditions of labor and migration for domestic workers—legal indenture, debt bondage, and isolation, for example—grant employers enormous, arbitrary authority. More generally, the absence of labor regulation and enforcement in domestic work makes these workers vulnerable. Notably, these insights did not arise while attempting to quantify the exact number of human-trafficking victims. Critically, my understanding of how and why trafficking occurs, that is, the exploitation of a person who had been somehow coerced into or deceived about their situation, emerged from on-the-ground qualitative research, including interviews and participant observation. How trafficking or forced labor occurs should be as much a focus of research as the determination of the exact number of victims.

Within their structural and social context, employers choose to either maximize or mitigate the authority they have over domestic workers, to become exploiters or anti-exploiters. Interestingly, both exploiters and anti-exploiters use moral justifications for their actions. Anti-exploiters insist on following democratic principles of freedom, despite social pressure to exploit workers. Take the case of Beatrice, who refused to subject her domestic worker to debt bondage, rejecting the advice of the recruitment agency. A different logic of moral justification allows exploiters to engage in forced labor without moral compunction. From Dubai to Singapore to the United States, with some variation, exploiters all exhibit an employer savior complex and a sense of pernicious ignorance.

I find that most domestic employers who engage in forced labor or trafficking truly believe that their horrible treatment of domestic workers represents a better option than whatever these workers had experienced prior to their employment. Tizon imagined that Pulido's enslavement likely saved her from a life of abject poverty—a logic supported by cultural defenders of her enslavement. But would the workers agree? Paying below-market wages is unacceptable, even if that wage is much more than what an employee could have earned prior to migration. This injustice is often coupled with the indignity of eating leftovers or the dehumanization of being assigned endless tasks by an employer who feels they own your time. Not a single worker I met in Singapore felt that their subjection to debt bondage was justified. Likewise, not a single worker I met in Dubai was satisfied with below-market wages. Employers know this, which is why some choose to isolate workers and deny them days off; they don't want the worker to find out that their friend in a neighboring household earns much more and then come back and ask for a raise.

If forced labor is one of the most pressing crimes of the twenty-first century, how do we address it? How do we mitigate the likelihood of its occurrence? We can ask the same of human trafficking. Advocates, domestic employers, and domestic workers have taken a variety of approaches. A wide range of key actors have recognized and attended to the problem of human trafficking and forced labor, including nation-states that deploy migrant domestic workers, such as Indonesia and the Philippines; nation-states that receive them, including the United Arab Emirates and Singapore; multilateral organizations such as the United Nations, International Labour Organization, and International Organization for Migration; international nongovernmental organizations such as Migrant-Rights.org and Human Rights Watch; advocacy groups in the United States such as the National Domestic Workers Alliance, along with its local constituents the Coalition for Humane Immigrant Rights of Los Angeles, Pilipino Workers Center of Southern California, and Damayan Migrant Workers in New York City, among others; domestic employer networks such as Hand in Hand in the United States; and finally, a wide range of academics, including anthropologists, economists, geographers, philosophers, and sociologists.

Each of these constituents offers different solutions, but a three-pronged strategy has emerged from their efforts: employer punishment, formal recognition of the occupation, and moral advocacy toward the greater valuation of domestic work. The punitive approach begins with anti-trafficking laws that national governments across the globe have been implementing since the United Nations passed the Protocol to Prevent, Suppress, and Punish Trafficking in Persons in 2000. The United States has passed at least nine key pieces of legislation on human trafficking, beginning with the Trafficking Victims Protection Act of 2000, which heightened the capacity of federal prosecutors to punish traffickers. In Singapore, the parliament instituted the Prevention of Human Trafficking Act of 2014, which imposed a possible penalty of S$100,000, up to 10 years of imprisonment, and caning for those convicted of human trafficking. In the United Arab Emirates, Federal Law No. 51 of 2006 and its amendments in Federal Law No. 1 of 2015 criminalized human and sex trafficking with a prescribed penalty of at least 5 years of incarceration. But punitive laws in these three countries have not deterred domestic employers from committing forced-labor crimes, in part because anti-trafficking advocates are more focused on sex-trafficking offenses. But these laws have also fallen short because domestic workers are isolated in the home, which shields employers from scrutiny.

Another strategy involves the formal recognition of the otherwise informal occupation of domestic work. The ILO leads the way in the implementation of legal recognition, and accordingly protection, of domestic workers. In 2011, the ILO passed Convention 189, otherwise known as the Convention Concerning Decent Work for Domestic Workers. This convention aimed to regulate domestic employment across the globe by establishing international standards, including the provision of a mandatory weekly rest day, adequate food, decent accommodations, and various safety measures. As of early 2024, 37 countries had ratified this convention.

Yet none of the key destinations for domestic workers has ratified it. Canada, Israel, Denmark, the Netherlands, the Gulf Cooperation Council countries in the Middle East, Malaysia, Taiwan, and Singapore have not passed the convention. Instead, they have at most extended an olive branch by selectively enacting principles of the convention with laws that aim to provide domestic workers with greater protection. For example, the Kingdom of Saudi Arabia, Singapore, and United Arab Emirates have all implemented a mandatory day off.

Even before the passage of ILO Convention 189, countries such as Ethiopia, Indonesia, and the Philippines had implemented bold measures to ensure the well-being of migrant domestic workers. Notably, these measures were intended not only to minimize risks for their citizens but also to maximize the economic returns they could squeeze from the migrants' labor. Each of these countries has sought to establish minimum standards of employment, including a monthly minimum wage, through memoranda of understanding with migrant-receiving countries. They have also instituted various empowerment projects and protectionist policies, including compulsory predeparture orientation seminars. Migrant-sending states use these seminars to educate domestic workers about minimum labor standards, including a minimum wage for countries without one, maximum hours of work per day, and boundaries of sexual harassment. There is value in these seminars. This is where domestic workers learn of otherwise nonexistent labor standards and acquire a benchmark that they can then use to gauge their labor conditions. Take the case of the recommended minimum wage of $400 per month implemented by the Philippine government. As I saw in Dubai, some workers who earned less than $400 were compelled to raise the issue with their employers and managed to successfully secure a higher wage.

Supporting the efforts of the ILO and migrant-sending states are labor unions; nongovernmental organizations, including the international organization Human Rights Watch; regional advocacy group Migrant-Rights.org in the Arab region; and national advocacy groups Transient Workers Count Too in Singapore and National Domestic Workers Alliance in the United States. These organizations support legislative reform and the legal recognition of domestic work as an occupation. Nongovernmental organizations have primarily established a key supporting role by conducting investigative studies that document the ill treatment of domestic workers and by educating the public through reports and media awareness campaigns on human rights violations against domestic workers.

In the past decade, we have seen a dizzying number of reports released by advocacy groups, including from Human Rights Watch on domestic workers in Bahrain in 2012, United Arab Emirates in 2014, Oman in 2016, United Arab Emirates and Oman in 2017, and Lebanon in 2020. Their efforts create what we can describe as a moral discourse around domestic work that sets the baseline for what should be acceptable standards of employment. For instance, these reports use the denial of a day off as evidence of modern-day slavery. Advocacy groups also attempt to create change by lobbying for legal reform. Consider the pioneering work of the National Domestic Workers Alliance to create a Domestic Worker Bill of Rights. As a result of their efforts, there is now a minimum standard of employment for domestic workers in California, Connecticut, Hawaii, Illinois, Massachusetts, Nevada, New Mexico, New York, Oregon, and Virginia.

This work could not have been done without the support of domestic employers. Through formal advocacy organizations, domestic employers play a key role in the legal recognition of domestic work. Their cooperation was essential in the passage of ILO Convention 189 as well as the Domestic Worker Bill of Rights across the United States. Policymaking in the ILO follows a tripartite system that requires the support of not only governments and workers but also employers. The separate research of scholars Adelle Blackett and Jennifer Fish shows that moral accountability for the well-being of domestic workers explains why employer organizations went against their own interests and supported Convention 189. For employers, this convention includes provisions that could make paid domestic work more expensive, even unaffordable to some. One example: the push for minimum labor standards, which opens the door for the implementation of a minimum wage. In the United States, domestic workers (along with agricultural workers) were excluded from the Fair Labor Standards Act of 1938, which created the right to a minimum wage and overtime pay. It was not until 1974 that domestic workers were granted the right to a minimum wage and overtime pay, but child- and elderly-care workers were still excluded. The law was expanded again in 2015 to include care workers but not live-in care workers, who remain exempt from overtime pay. Some employers, however, are not completely supportive of these changes.

From the efforts of multilateral agencies, governments, and nongovernmental organizations, we have seen an explosion of laws that criminalize the abuse of domestic workers and set labor standards to ensure their better treatment in the workplace. Yet these laws have not successfully eliminated human trafficking, enslavement, or peonage. This is in part because migrant domestic workers have limited labor rights and thus cannot participate freely in the labor market. Because they cannot quit if unhappy with their labor conditions, migrant domestic workers must often accept even the worst of employers, including those that inflict criminal, inhumane treatment and forced labor.

Poor enforcement of these laws is also to blame. We see this clearly in the case of Canada, which is one of the few countries that include domestic workers in their general labor laws. Despite robust labor-protectionist laws, domestic workers in Canada have not been spared the worst treatment of employers. A former domestic worker named Clara, a 47-year-old Filipina migrant, articulated the problem when she complained, "What is the point of having laws if no one will implement them?" Clara suffered profoundly while she worked for a family who consistently fed her table scraps and little else. Most evenings, as Clara would watch them eat, she would pray that they would leave her something more substantial than the bones of the rotisserie chicken or the broth of the stew. After two years of continuous employment, she found herself malnourished and 30 pounds lighter than when she first arrived.

There are many domestic workers who can easily fall through the cracks of legal protection. It is not just Clara. Her situation tells us that the issue of human trafficking cannot be solved by laws alone. According to her, improving labor conditions for domestic workers requires not just policy protection but also greater understanding from employers. It is not equality she wants but empathy, she says. A group of economists led by Toman Barsbai from the University of Bristol in England share her sentiments. Recognizing the need for solutions other than public policy, his research team conducted a randomized experiment that measured the effects of social distance between employers and domestic workers. They recruited research participants in predeparture orientation seminars in the Philippines. They then had hundreds of domestic workers who were bound for Hong Kong and the Kingdom of Saudi Arabia offer their employer a small gift of a pack of dried mangoes during their initial meeting. They also had the worker leave a picture of their family in an area visible to employers. The gift and the picture were intended to ease social distance and humanize the workers. Indeed, they found that those who participated in the experiment were more likely to experience humane treatment and job satisfaction. Yet this study puts the onus on domestic workers to "teach" their employers to see them as humans. Is it possible for employers to treat domestic workers with dignity without a reminder, pressure, or the gift of a pack of mangoes?

This is a pressing question that at its core asks how employers can avoid the trap of becoming an unwitting trafficker or exploiter of domestic workers. To break the cycle of pernicious ignorance, employers must resist iniquitous employment structures. They must consciously become anti-exploiters. The first step is recognizing domestic workers' humanity, including their need for food, rest, leisure, and companionship.

Employers must also reject the employer savior complex. Instead of focusing on the good they have done for domestic workers, employers should recognize all that domestic workers have done for them. How do domestic workers ease the burdens of daily life? For example, do they enable employers to maximize their earning potential outside the home? In recognition, employers should consider providing their domestic workers with education assistance or retirement funds. These remunerations counter the informal nature of domestic work and the lack of retirement compensation.

Finally, employers should establish and stick to an employer contract. It is easy to be seduced by the convenience wrought by the subjugation of a domestic worker. Greed can get the better of us, especially if it remains undetected. What's the big deal, one might think, about asking a domestic worker to stay for 10 more minutes or do one more load of laundry? You might even be able to convince yourself that the worker doesn't mind; you are friends, after all. While that may be the case, the personal bond between employer and domestic worker does not override the market arrangement. The familiarity bred in the intimate space of the home can make it hard for a domestic worker to insist on payment for these extra minutes and tasks. But small favors can add up to a sizable amount of forced labor.

The United States–based employer network Hand in Hand suggests that employers enforce a contract that specifically outlines the labor conditions prior to the start of employment. It's critical that employers then stick to the terms of the contract—the set time and hours, holidays, duties and responsibilities, and wage rates, including a structured bonus and raise schema. While a contract might feel overly rigid, it's important that employers remember that for domestic workers, the home is their workplace.

Morals matter. Being an anti-exploiter means being thoughtful about your impact and rejecting the logic that "it was worse where they came from." One must instead measure labor conditions within the local context and provide a salary and benefits that are on par with recommended norms. In the United States, Hand in Hand offers resources to guide employers on how to determine fair labor conditions, including wages.

Yet sometimes this is not enough. What do you do when local norms arguably violate the human rights of the worker? This is the case in Singapore. When local norms fall short, aspiring anti-exploiters must resist the urge of pernicious ignorance. This requires that employers approach the management of domestic workers in a morally minded way as opposed to a profit-minded one. Instead of thinking about how much they can extract from a domestic worker, employers need to be vigilant about not taking advantage of their workers. While most employers I met in Singapore blindly imposed peonage, many did resist it, like Beatrice. Some employers equally split the agency fees with their domestic worker, while others covered all the fees the worker incurred for securing a job in their home.

Whether it's peonage in Singapore, the absence of a minimum wage in the United Arab Emirates, or legal indenture in the United States, it's clear that our standards must be higher than what is technically permitted by the law. This is why I urge employers to ultimately abide by moral standards. Being an anti-exploiter ultimately means having the moral wherewithal to bring dignity to the home as a workplace. It means ensuring that domestic work is not just decent work but also a path of upward mobility for those who take on the hard work of caring, cooking, and cleaning. It means recognizing that domestic workers play a key role in enabling others to thrive.

ACKNOWLEDGMENTS

THIS BOOK BENEFITED from the many discussions I had with my research collaborator, Rachel Silvey, and from the critical readings of earlier versions by Maria Cecilia Hwang, May Jeong, and Kritika Pandey, as well as in various workshops, including the Crime, Law and Punishment Workshop in New York University's Department of Sociology and the Gender, Theory and Power working group sponsored by Northwestern University's Department of Sociology. I thank the organizers, Lynne Haney and Ann Orloff, as well as the participants for their invaluable feedback. This book was made possible by the support of Karl Jacoby and my editors at W. W. Norton: Tom Mayer, Sasha Levitt, and YJ Wang. Data used in this book draw from a research study on domestic workers that was funded by the National Science Foundation (SES-1346750) and the Social Science and Humanities Research Council of Canada (file no. 895-2012-1021; PI: Ito Peng).

GLOSSARY

Forced Labor According to the International Labour Organization 1930 Forced Labour Convention, forced or compulsory labor refers to "all work or service which is exacted from any person under the menace of any penalty and for which the said person has not offered himself voluntarily."

Human Trafficking Defined in the 2000 United Nations Protocol to Prevent, Suppress and Punish Trafficking in Persons Especially Women and Children, supplementing the United Nations Convention Against Transnational Organized Crime, "'trafficking in persons' shall mean the recruitment, transportation, transfer, harbouring or receipt of persons, by means of the threat or use of force or other forms of coercion, of abduction, of fraud, of deception, of the abuse of power or of a position of vulnerability or of the giving or receiving of payments or benefits to achieve the consent of a person having control over another person, for the purpose of exploitation. Exploitation shall include, at a minimum, the exploitation of the prostitution of others or other forms of sexual exploitation, forced labour or services, slavery or practices similar to slavery, servitude or the removal of organs."

Modern-Day Slavery Modern-day slavery, according to Kevin Bales, refers to "the total control of one person [the slave] by another [the slaveholder or slaveholders] for the purpose of economic exploitation."

Peonage Peonage, otherwise known as *debt labor* or *debt bondage*, refers to the pledge of a person's services as security for the repayment of a debt or other obligation.

Servitude Servitude refers to a state of a person's subjection as a servant, either voluntary or involuntary.

Slavery As defined in the League of Nations Slavery Convention of 1926, slavery is "the status or condition of a person over whom any or all of the powers attaching to the right of ownership are exercised."

NOTES

INTRODUCTION: THE TRAFFICKER NEXT DOOR

1 *The Real Mo Farah*: Leo Burley, dir., *The Real Mo Farah* (Atomized Studios, 2022).
3 **1904 International Agreement**: International Agreement for the Suppression of the "White Slave Traffic," May 18, 1904, 35 Stat. 1979, League of Nations Treaty Series 496.
3 **Only in 2000**: UN General Assembly, Resolution 55/25 A, Protocol to Prevent, Suppress and Punish Trafficking in Persons Especially Women and Children, Supplementing the United Nations Convention Against Transnational Organized Crime, A/RES/55/25 (November 15, 2000).
3 **denied Farah's accusations**: Graeme Culliford, "The Mo 'Trafficker': First Picture of Woman Who Brought Mo Farah into UK with Falsified Visa," *Sun*, July 16, 2022.
3 **"My mum said that she risked"**: Fariha Karim, "Farah Was No Slave—He Did Chores Like the Rest of Us, Says 'Brother,'" *Times*, July 18, 2022.
4 **"raised daughters"**: Elizabeth Hordge-Freeman, *Second-Class Daughters: Black Brazilian Women and Informal Adoption as Modern Slavery* (Cambridge University Press, 2022).
4 *restavek*: Jean-Robert Cadet, *Restavec: From Haitian Slave Child to Middle-Class American* (University of Texas Press, 1998).
4 **Ghana**: Peace Mamle Tetteh, "Child Domestic Labor in Accra: Opportunity and Empowerment or Perpetuation of Gender Inequality?," *Ghana Studies* 14 (2011): 163–89.
4 **the movie *Taken***: Pierre Morel, dir., *Taken* (20th Century Studios, 2009).
4 **Cadena brothers**: Anthony DeStefano, *The War on Human Trafficking: U.S. Policy Assessed* (Rutgers University Press, 2007), 1–8.

5   grown in the past few decades: Kate Hodal, "One in 200 People Is a Slave. Why?," *Guardian*, February 25, 2019.
5   **1926 Slavery Convention**: Convention to Suppress the Slave Trade and Slavery, League of Nations, September 25, 1926.
5   **defines enslavement**: Kevin Bales, *Disposable People: New Slavery in the Global Economy* (University of California Press, 1999), 6.
5   **"contract slavery"**: Kevin Bales, "Expendable People: Slavery in the Age of Globalization," *Journal of International Affairs* 53, no. 2 (2000): 462–64.
5   **forced labor**: International Labour Organization, Convention 029, Forced Labour Convention, 1930.
5   **CNN reports**: Ricky Martin, "Stop the Scourge of Child Trafficking," *CNN*, November 3, 2011.
5   *Trafficking in Persons Report*: U.S. Department of State, *Trafficking in Persons Report* (U.S. Government Printing Office, 2011).
5   **speech by former U.S. Secretary**: "Secretary Antony J. Blinken at the Release of the 2023 Trafficking in Persons Report," U.S. Department of State, press release, June 15, 2023.
5   **But the 27-million figure**: Kevin Bales, *Understanding Global Slavery: A Reader* (University of California Press, 2005), 101–2; Kevin Bales, "International Labor Standards: Quality of Information and Measures of Progress in Combating Forced Labor," *Comparative Labor Law and Policy Journal* 24, no. 2 (2004): 343.
6   **Bales himself has turned to**: Kevin Bales, "The Methodology Behind the Global Slavery Index," *Guardian*, October 17, 2013.
6   **29.8 million in 2013**: *The Global Slavery Index 2013* (Walk Free Foundation), 6.
6   **50 million in 2023**: *The Global Slavery Index 2023* (Walk Free Foundation), i.
6   **Anne Gallagher**: Anne Gallagher, "What's Wrong with the Global Slavery Index?," *Anti-Trafficking Review* 8 (2017): 90–112.
6   **24.9 million individuals**: International Labour Organization, *Global Estimates of Modern Slavery* (International Labour Organization, 2017), 7.
6   **16 million persons**: *Global Estimates of Modern Slavery*, 2017, 8.
6   **survey of 71,000 individuals**: *Global Estimates of Modern Slavery*, 2017, 9.
7   **80 percent**: Heather Clawson et al., *Human Trafficking Into and Within the United States: A Review of the Literature* (U.S. Department of Health and Human Services Office of the Assistant Secretary for Planning and Evaluation, August 2009), 4.

7 **criminologist Sheldon Zhang:** Sheldon Zhang, "Beyond the 'Natasha' Story: A Review and Critique of Current Research on Sex Trafficking," *Global Crime* 10, no. 3 (2009): 178–95.

7 **Sociologist Katharine Donato:** Katharine Donato and Donna Gabaccia, *Gender and International Migration: From the Slavery Era to the Global Age* (Russell Sage Foundation, 2015), 36.

7 **white male heroism:** Carole Vance, "Innocence and Experience: Melodramatic Narratives of Sex Trafficking and Their Consequences for Law and Policy," *History of the Present* 2, no. 2 (Fall 2012): 200–218; Ruby Platt, "Modern-Day Slavery? American Male Saviorism in Anti–Sex Trafficking Efforts," unpublished paper for Princeton University seminar, 2023.

7 *Sound of Freedom*: Alejandro Monteverde, dir., *Sound of Freedom* (Angel Studios, 2023).

7 **writings of men such as Bales:** Bales, *Disposable People*; Bales, "Expendable People"; Bales, *Understanding Global Slavery*.

8 **Jo Doezema:** Jo Doezema, *Sex Slaves and Discourse Masters: The Construction of Trafficking* (Zed Books, 2013).

8 **Laura Lammasniemi:** Laura Lammasniemi, "Anti–White Slavery Legislation and Its Legacies in England," *Anti-Trafficking Review* 9 (2017): 64–76.

8 **Modern-day calls for "heroes":** For *Trafficking in Persons Report*, see http://www.tipheroes.org/the-heroes/.

8 **"moral panic":** Stanley Cohen, *Folk Devils and Moral Panics* (Routledge, 2011).

8 **inaccessibility of victims:** Examples of studies that justify their small sample of workers vulnerable to trafficking with the argument of inaccessibility include, in Malaysia, Olivia Killias, *Follow the Maid: Domestic Worker Migration in and from Indonesia* (NIAS Press, 2017), and in the United Arab Emirates, Cawo Abdi, *The Elusive Jannah: The Somali Diaspora and a Borderless Muslim Identity* (University of Minnesota Press, 2015).

8 **UN Office on Drugs and Crime:** Rhacel Salazar Parreñas, *Illicit Flirtations: Labor, Migration, and Sex Trafficking in Tokyo* (Stanford University Press, 2011), 6.

8 **Ronald Weitzer:** Ronald Weitzer, "New Directions in Research on Human Trafficking," *Annals of the American Academy of Political and Social Science* 653 (May 2014): 6–24.

9 **nightlife industry of Tokyo:** Parreñas, *Illicit Flirtations*.

9 **victims of forced prostitution:** U.S. Department of State, *Trafficking in Persons Report*, 2004, 14.
9 **"stripped of their passports":** *Trafficking in Persons Report*, 2004, 14.
9 **criticized by scholars:** Sally Engle Merry, *The Seductions of Quantification: Measuring Human Rights, Gender Violence, and Sex Trafficking* (University of Chicago Press, 2016).
9 **"global sheriff":** Janie Chuang, "The United States as Global Sheriff: Using Unilateral Sanctions to Combat Human Trafficking," *Michigan Journal of International Law* 27, no. 2 (2006): 437–94.
9 **it didn't include itself:** Kate Noftsinger, "U.S. Finally Includes Itself in Human Trafficking Report," *Ms.*, July 22, 2010.
9 **In initial publications:** U.S. Department of State, *Trafficking in Persons Report*, 2001, introduction; U.S. Department of State, *Trafficking in Persons Report*, 2002, introduction.
10 **U.S. Government Accountability Office:** U.S. Government Accountability Office, "Human Trafficking: Better Data, Strategy, and Reporting Needed to Enhance U.S. Antitrafficking Efforts Abroad," *Trends in Organized Crime* 10 (2006): 20, 21.
10 **80,000 Filipina entertainers:** Parreñas, *Illicit Flirtations*, 4.
11 **"structural vulnerability":** Philippe Bourgois, Seth Holmes, Kim Sue, and James Quesada, "Structural Vulnerability: Operationalizing the Concept to Address Health Disparities in Clinical Care," *Academic Medicine* 92, no. 3 (March 2017): 299–307.
11 **Denise Brennan's work:** Denise Brennan, *Life Interrupted: Trafficking into Forced Labor in the United States* (Duke University Press, 2014).
12 **67 million domestic workers globally:** Maria Gallotti, *Migrant Domestic Workers Across the World: Global and Regional Estimates* (International Labour Organization, 2015), 1; International Labour Organization, *ILO Global Estimates on Migrant Workers* (International Labour Organization, 2015); International Labour Organization, *Making Decent Work a Reality for Domestic Workers* (International Labour Organization, 2021).
12 **2022 report by the ILO:** International Labour Organization, Walk Free, and International Organization for Migration, *Global Estimates of Modern Slavery: Forced Labour and Forced Marriage* (International Labour Organization, 2022), 31.
12 **This is a drop:** International Labour Organization, Walk Free, and International Organization for Migration, *Global Estimates of Modern Slavery:*

Forced Labour and Forced Marriage (International Labour Organization, 2017), 11.

12 **similar methodology:** ILO publications use different methodologies. Some have employed questionable methods, as I pointed out earlier, which is why it is important to pay attention to the methods used in each study. ILO research on domestic work uses more reliable methods and draws from national data sources.

13 **standard employment conditions:** Rhacel Salazar Parreñas, *Unfree: Migrant Domestic Work in Arab States* (Stanford University Press, 2022), 27–30.

13 **case of au pairs:** "Protections for Domestic Workers: Spotlight on Au Pairs," National Domestic Workers Alliance, April 2016.

13 **J-1 Exchange Visitor Program:** This program was created as part of the Fulbright-Hays Act of 1961, or the Mutual Educational and Cultural Exchange Act.

13 **U.S. Information Agency:** Janie Chuang, "The U.S. Au Pair Program: Labor Exploitation and the Myth of Cultural Exchange," *Harvard Journal of Law and Gender* 36 (2013): 275.

13 **largest group of participants:** U.S. Department of State J-1 Visa Au Pair Program, Total Au Pairs by Country for 2015 (online).

14 **"exchange visitors":** Chuang, "U.S. Au Pair Program."

14 **Ashish Gupta:** Shae Healey, "In Unsafe Hands," *Willamette Week*, October 25, 2011.

14 **Most au pairs can be found:** Alex Nowrasteh, "New State Department Regulations Could End the Au Pair Program," *Cato at Liberty* (blog), Cato Institute, November 21, 2023.

14 **artificially low wage rate of $4.35:** This is no longer the case in Massachusetts. In 2019, the U.S. Court of Appeals for the First Circuit ruled against the prevailing wage compensation for au pairs, which is based on the $7.25 federal minimum wage, and required host families in Massachusetts to calculate the earnings of au pairs based on the higher state minimum wage rate of $15. Vanessa Romo, "Au Pair Sponsor Agencies Settle Wage Lawsuit, Offer $65.5 Million in Back Pay," *NPR*, January 9, 2019.

14 **Kingdom of Saudi Arabia:** Saudi Arabia: Ministerial Decision No. 399 of 2007/1428H on Housing Conditions for Workers, Gulf Labour Markets and Migration, 2007.

14 **Adding to au pairs' vulnerability:** Polaris Project and National Domestic

Workers Alliance, *Human Trafficking at Home: Labor Trafficking of Domestic Workers* (Polaris Project, 2019), 45–46; Zack Kopplin, "They Think We Are Slaves," *Politico*, March 27, 2017.

15 **Deportation is a risk:** Personal interviews and also see Kopplin, "They Think We Are Slaves."

15 **migrant labor regimes:** Rhacel Salazar Parreñas, *Servants of Globalization: Migration and Domestic Work*, 2nd ed. (Stanford University Press, 2015), 18–25.

15 **As documented by organizations:** Polaris Project and National Domestic Workers Alliance, *Human Trafficking at Home*. Also see Kopplin, "They Think We Are Slaves."

16 **"white-savior industrial complex":** Teju Cole, "The White-Savior Industrial Complex," *Atlantic*, March 21, 2012.

17 **Harit "Potee" Saluja:** "Indian Immigrant Servants Accuse Long Island Family of Slavery," *CBS New York*, May 20, 2011.

18 **slavery as a benevolent institution:** John C. Calhoun, *Speeches of John C. Calhoun: Delivered in the Congress of the United States from 1811 to the Present Time* (New York: Harper's & Brothers, 1843), 222–26.

18 **slavery as providing humane conditions:** Drew Gilpin Faust, *James Henry Hammond and the Old South* (Louisiana State University Press, 1985).

18 **Orientalism:** Edward Said, *Orientalism* (Pantheon Books, 1978).

18 **"adopt" children of poorer relatives:** Belen T. G. Medina, *The Filipino Family*, 2nd ed. (U. P. Diliman Press, 2001), 19.

19 **"pernicious ignorance":** Kristie Dotson, "Tracking Epistemic Violence, Tracking Practices of Silencing," *Hypatia* 26, no. 2 (2011): 238.

19 **ideology of female domesticity:** Medina, *Filipino Family*, 140–44; Rhacel Salazar Parreñas, *The Force of Domesticity: Filipina Migrants and Globalization* (New York University Press, 2008), 8–9.

20 **coca plantations in Colombia:** Luz Estella Nagle and Juan Manuel Zarama, "Taking Responsibility Under International Law: Human Trafficking and Colombia's Venezuelan Migration Crisis," *University of Miami Inter-American Law Review* 53, no. 2 (2022): 59.

20 **Burmese fishermen:** Alastair Leithead, "Burmese 'Slavery' Fishermen Are Trafficked and Abused," *BBC News*, April 25, 2011.

20 **Syrians fleeing to Germany:** Sean Flynn, "The Deadly Journey Faced by Refugees in Europe," *GQ*, December 16, 2015.

CHAPTER 1: A MODERN-DAY AMERICAN SLAVE

21 a 2017 *Atlantic* cover article: Alex Tizon, "My Family's Slave," *Atlantic*, June 2017.
23 Orlando Patterson: Orlando Patterson, *Slavery and Social Death: A Comparative Study* (Harvard University Press, 1982), 1–14.
24 Pulido's story sparked intense debate: I followed these debates on X (formerly Twitter).
25 Espousing a cultural defense: Vicente Rafael, "Lola's Resistant Dignity: Reading 'My Family's Slave' in the Context of Philippine History," *Atlantic*, May 31, 2017.
26 practice of bartering children: Hordge-Freeman, *Second-Class Daughters*.
27 experts on domestic work: Mary Romero, *Maid in the U.S.A.* (Routledge, 2002); Judith Rollins, *Between Women: Domestics and Their Employers* (Temple University Press, 1985).
27 manumission was as low: Patterson, *Slavery and Social Death*, 273, for rates in the U.S. South, South Africa, Jamaica, and Colombia; 287, for Curaçao; and 274, for Muslim Spain.
28 I decided to turn: Helping me identify where to locate relatives in the Philippines is Lian Buan, "Eudocia Pulido Had Hopes, Dreams, and Fears Too," *Rappler*, May 24, 2017.
30 Despite the story's widespread coverage: Buan, "Eudocia Pulido Had Hopes"; Rachel Martin, "In Telling Lola's Story, a Journalist Reveals a Family Secret," *NPR*, May 16, 2017.
31 "natal alienation": Patterson, *Slavery and Social Death*, 1–14.
34 a culture of servitude: Medina, *Filipino Family*, 19–20.
35 estimated 25 percent of children: Rhacel Parreñas, *Children of Global Migration: Transnational Families and Gendered Woes* (Stanford University Press, 2005), 12.
35 "middlewomen": Joanna Dreby, *Divided by Borders: Mexican Migrants and Their Children* (University of California Press, 2010), 145–77.
36 slavery is more common: International Labour Organization, Walk Free, and International Organization for Migration, *Global Estimates of Modern Slavery*, 2022, 3.
36 two million domestic workers: Asha Banerjee, Katherine deCourcy, Kyle Moore, and Julia Wolfe, "Domestic Workers Chartbook 2022," Economic Policy Institute, November 22, 2022.

36 **According to the anti-trafficking organization:** Polaris Project and National Domestic Workers Alliance, *Human Trafficking at Home*, 4.
36 **National Human Trafficking Hotline:** *Human Trafficking at Home*, 4.
36 **foreign nationals:** *Human Trafficking at Home*, 25.
37 **Many victims were trafficked:** *Human Trafficking at Home*, 23.
37 **worker whose visa she sponsored:** In the United States, an employer can sponsor an unskilled worker for permanent residency if it is for a job that citizens of the country cannot or refuse to perform. Domestic work is one such job. The government allocates 10,000 of such visas to unskilled workers annually.
38 **"contract slavery":** Bales, "Expendable People," 462–64.
39 **shortage of medical professionals:** Catherine Ceniza Choy, *Empire of Care: Nursing and Migration in Filipino American History* (Duke University Press, 2003).
39 **criminalization of undocumented workers:** Tanya Golash-Boza, "Notes from the Field: The Criminalization of Undocumented Migrants; Legalities and Realities," *Societies Without Borders* 5, no. 1 (2010): 81–90.
40 **Researcher Denise Brennan argues:** Brennan, *Life Interrupted*.
40 **This includes Fedelina Lugasan:** Jonah Valdez and Ruby Gonzales, "First Robbed of Freedom by Enslavement, Then Robbed of Life by Coronavirus," *Los Angeles Daily News*, October 31, 2020; Paulina Velasco, "The Rescue," *UnFictional*, Bob Carlson, host, *KCRW*, July 4, 2020.
41 **case of Irma Martinez:** United States v. Calimlim, 07-1112, 07-1113, 07-1281 (7th Cir. 2008).
41 **Abdel Nassar Eid Youssef Ibrahim:** Sara Lin, "Pair Admit Keeping Girl, 12, as a Slave," *Los Angeles Times*, June 30, 2006.
41 **case of Sandra Luz Bearden:** Bearden v. The State of Texas, 04-04-00019-CR (49th Judicial District Court 2003).
42 **Cuban migrants in Miami:** Alejandro Portes, "The Social Origins of the Cuban Enclave Economy of Miami," *Sociological Perspectives* 30, no. 4 (1987): 340–72.
42 **Frederick Douglass:** Frederick Douglass, *Narrative of the Life of Frederick Douglass* (1845; Random House, 2005), 99.
43 **Marilou Ilagan:** Parreñas, *Servants of Globalization*, 15–17.
44 **In fact, Nana Ebia:** Buan, "Eudocia Pulido Had Hopes."
45 **A survey I conducted:** Jennifer Nazareno, Rhacel Parreñas, and Yu Kang Fan, "Can I Ever Retire? Making a Case for the 'Retireable Wage' of Elderly Caregivers in Los Angeles," Pilipino Workers Center, 2014.

45 **survey conducted by the National Domestic Workers Alliance:** Linda Burnham and Nik Theodore, *Home Economics: The Invisible and Unregulated World of Domestic Work*, National Domestic Workers Alliance, xi.

45 **only 9 percent of employers:** Rhacel Salazar Parreñas, "The Aging of Migrant Domestic Workers," *American Prospect*, October 20, 2020.

46 **article in *People* magazine:** Rose Minutaglio, "Wife of Late Writer Who Revealed He Was Raised by Family's Secret Slave Speaks Out: 'It Was Painful, I Was Horrified,'" *People*, May 19, 2017.

46 **Albert Tizon:** Boying Pimentel, "Alex Tizon's Final Act of Courage," *Philippine Inquirer*, May 23, 2017.

46 **Take the case of Lugasan:** Valdez and Gonzales, "First Robbed of Freedom"; Velasco, "Rescue."

CHAPTER 2: THE RISKS MIGRANTS TAKE

52 **3,000 prospective migrant domestic workers:** Estimate calculated by author based on number of classes administered and the size of the classes.

52 **As one of the largest source countries:** Parreñas, *Unfree*.

53 **recruitment agents deceive:** Antoinette Vlieger, "Domestic Workers in Saudi Arabia and the Emirates: Trafficking Victims?," *International Migration* 50, no. 6 (2011): 180–94.

53 **American anthropologist Andrew Gardner:** Andrew Gardner, "Why Do They Keep Coming? Labor Migrants in the Persian Gulf States," in *Migrant Labor in the Persian Gulf*, ed. Mehran Kamrava and Zahra Babar (C. Hurst & Co., 2012), 41–58.

53 **Sending states like the Philippines:** Parreñas, *Unfree*, 53–61.

54 **Instead, domestic workers go:** Parreñas, *Servants of Globalization*, 3.

54 **cost of their migration:** Elsewhere migrant domestic workers must pay with the cost fluctuating across countries. The higher the average salary in the destination then the higher the cost of migration. In Singapore, a prospective domestic worker from the Philippines must pay a minimum of 3 months' worth of their salary, which would total around $1,200; 7 months of their salary, or around $4,480, in Hong Kong; 12 months of their salary, or $7,416, in Taiwan; and significantly more in other countries, including Canada, where it would cost at least $10,000 to $12,000 to secure a labor contract. Most, if not all, accrue debt to cover these expenses.

54 **27 percent:** Gallotti, *Migrant Domestic Workers*, 2.

58 **South Asian workers:** Natasha Iskander, *Does Skill Make Us Human? Migrant Workers in 21st-Century Qatar and Beyond* (Princeton University Press, 2021); Greg Bishop, "In Building This World Cup, They 'Fulfilled the Beauty of Qatar. But There Is No Happiness for Us,'" *Sports Illustrated*, December 16, 2022.

58 **Myanmar nationals:** Shannon Service and Becky Palmstrom, "Confined to a Thai Fishing Boat, for Three Years," *NPR*, June 19, 2012.

58 **"hopeful uncertainty":** Anna Triandafyllidou, "The Migration Archipelago: Social Navigation and Migrant Agency," *International Migration* 57, no. 1. (2019): 11.

59 **50,000 Americans living in Dubai:** The estimated number draws from online investment blogs written about expatriate life in the United Arab Emirates, with many providing the estimated count of 50,000. Examples are Off the Mrkt and Imperial Citizenship.

60 **without a minimum wage:** This is more than the 500 dirhams, or $135, recommended by the Bangladeshi government as a minimum wage for its citizens.

61 **residence visa:** The residence visa is distinct and separate from the tourist visa Sanaya purchased to enter the country.

62 **pregnancy outside of marriage:** Parreñas, *Unfree*, 37; Isabel Debre, "After UAE Law Change, Out-of-Wedlock Babies Still in Shadows," *AP News*, December 13, 2021.

62 **Abortion is illegal:** See Article 391 in the UAE government website of legislations, https://uaelegislation.gov.ae/en/legislations/1529. The government revisited its abortion law in June 2024, under Cabinet Resolution No. (44) of 2024, allowing women to obtain permission for an abortion on a case-by-case basis.

62 **"contract substitution":** International Labour Organization, Walk Free, and International Organization for Migration, *Global Estimates of Modern Slavery*, 2022, 82.

63 ***kafala* system:** In 2017, the United Arab Emirates restructured its sponsorship system of domestic workers and allowed live-out employment. These workers remain a minority. High costs of housing deter most from taking this option. Employers also maintain a greater preference for live-in workers. Both live-in and live-out domestic workers remain subject to the kafala. Parreñas, *Unfree*, 4–5.

64 **similar system of governance:** Qatar revisited its kafala system and introduced reform measures in 2020. Migrant workers, including domestic

workers, no longer need their employer's permission to quit their job. But domestic workers are still limited to live-in employment in one household and are required to give their employer a minimum of one month's notice to legally terminate their contract. Abused domestic workers are not exempt from the one-month requirement. Other countries, including the United Arab Emirates and the Kingdom of Saudi Arabia, excluded domestic workers from any reforms in kafala law. Overview of kafala is provided by the Council on Foreign Relations. See Kali Robinson, "What is the Kafala System?," Council on Foreign Relations, November 18, 2022.

64 **Live-in Caregiver Program:** Abigail Bakan and Daiva Stasiulis, "Foreign Domestic Worker Policy in Canada and the Social Boundaries of Modern Citizenship," in *Not One of the Family: Foreign Domestic Workers in Canada*, ed. Abigail Bakan and Daiva Stasiulis (University of Toronto Press, 1997), 29–52.

65 **reformed the program in 2014:** "Major Reforms to Caregiver Program Announced by Canadian Government," *CIC News*, November 5, 2014.

65 **kafala-like conditions:** Parreñas, *Unfree*, 27–30.

66 **"structural violence":** Pardis Mahdavi writes on the structural violence confronting domestic workers in Dubai in *Gridlock: Labor, Migration and Human Trafficking in Dubai* (Stanford University Press); Johan Galtung, "Violence, Peace, and Peace Research," *Journal of Peace Research* 6, no. 3 (1969): 167–91.

66 **According to Human Rights Watch:** Human Rights Watch, *"I Already Bought You": Abuse and Exploitation of Female Migrant Domestic Workers in the United Arab Emirates* (Human Rights Watch, 2014).

66 **Southeast Asia is home:** Gallotti, *Migrant Domestic Workers*, 2.

74 **anthropologist Nicole Constable:** Nicole Constable, *Maid to Order in Hong Kong: Stories of Migrant Workers*, 2nd ed. (Cornell University Press, 2007), 95, 102–3, 196.

75 **World Cup:** "Qatar: Six Months Post–World Cup, Migrant Workers Suffer," Human Rights Watch, June 16, 2023.

75 **Qatar:** On September 8, 2020, Qatar introduced significant labor reforms to the kafala by allowing migrant laborers to change jobs without the consent of their employer prior to the end of their labor contract. Yet they are still bound to working solely for their sponsor.

75 **H-2B visas:** The H-2B is a nonimmigrant visa program that allows employers to temporarily hire nonimmigrants to perform

nonagricultural labor. Migrants can work only for their sponsor. For a general history of the H2 program, including agricultural workers, see Cindy Hahamovitch, *No Man's Land: Jamaican Guestworkers in America and the Global History of Deportable Labor* (Princeton University Press, 2011).

75 **mechanical engineers:** For a general description of visa requirements and restrictions in the Kingdom of Saudi Arabia, see the government webpage on employment visas at https://www.saudiembassy.net/employment-visa.

75 **Saudi Arabia:** Since reforms to the kafala in March 2021, migrant workers (except for domestic and farm workers) in the Kingdom of Saudi Arabia can change jobs without the consent of employers after the completion of one year of employment. However, they are still bound to working solely for their sponsor.

75 **H-1B visa:** This is a temporary nonimmigrant visa category reserved for highly educated foreign professionals. Holders of this visa can transition to permanent residency, unlike unskilled migrant workers with H-2A or H-2B visas.

75 **high-tech firm:** Amy Bhatt, *High-Tech Housewives: Indian IT Workers, Gendered Labor and Transmigrations* (University of Washington Press, 2018).

75 **nurses under contract:** Contracts for foreign nurses petitioned by hospitals include a penalty clause requiring them to pay upwards of $25,000 if they leave their jobs early. Though a federal court in 2019 ruled that this penalty violates human trafficking laws, this practice continues.

75 **difficult . . . to quit their job:** Shannon Pettypiece, "'Indentured Servitude': Nurses Hit with Hefty Debt When Trying to Leave Hospitals," *NBC News*, March 12, 2023; and Bill Heltzel, "Filipino RNs Claim Glen Island Nursing Home Exploited Immigration Status," *Westfair Business Journal*, December 7, 2023.

75 **less-than-ideal work conditions:** See, for example, Amy Bhatt, *High-Tech Housewives*, and Pallavi Banerjee, *The Opportunity Trap: High-Skilled Workers, Indian Families, and the Failures of the Dependent Visa Program* (New York University Press, 2022).

75 **lottery system:** Bhatt, *High-Tech Housewives*, 20–22.

75 **separate studies:** Banerjee, *Opportunity Trap*; Bhatt, *High-Tech Housewives*.

76 *indentured mobility*: Parreñas, *Illicit Flirtations*, 7.

76 **sacrifice their freedom:** I introduce the concept of indentured mobility in my book *Illicit Flirtations*.

76 **"positive liberty"**: John Christman, "Liberalism and Individual Positive Freedom," *Ethics* 101, no. 2 (1991): 343–59.

CHAPTER 3: EXPLOITERS OF FORCED LABOR

77 **12 hours per day:** In 2014, the government of the United Arab Emirates gave domestic workers the right to eight continuous hours of rest per day and a mandatory rest day per week. Federal Decree-Law No. 9 of 2022 Concerning Domestic Workers, Article 9, United Arab Emirates.

78 **240,000 expatriates from Great Britain:** This is an estimated count frequently cited in the media. See Mohammed Sinan Siyech, "Understanding British Migration to the UAE," *Middle East Monitor*, July 15, 2024.

81 **bomb shelter:** This was mandated by the Civil Defense Shelter Act and prompted by the Gulf War in 1991.

81 **salaries of domestic workers vary:** Figures based on interviews with employment agency staff as well as observation of salary scales posted on the walls of different agencies.

85 **Employers' Orientation Programme:** This program is described on the website of Singapore's Ministry of Manpower under "Employers' Orientation Programme (EOP)."

85 **The course and the exam:** Based on participation observation and completion of the mandatory employer course.

86 **mismatched placement:** Though it is easy to assume this employer would be impossible to please, the domestic worker who replaced Jonna worked out splendidly.

87 **Anthropologist Nicole Constable:** Constable, *Maid to Order in Hong Kong*, 74–76.

90 **right to a weekly day off:** Description of minimum labor conditions, including days off, is available in the Ministry of Manpower website under "Employer's Guide: Migrant Domestic Worker."

90 **compensating someone $13.50:** This amount should be easily affordable for any member of the middle class in Singapore, where there are 245,600 migrant workers employed as domestic workers. In Singapore, the median monthly salary for full-time work is S$4,534, which in U.S. dollars would be $3,371.

90 **As of 2023:** See Ministry of Manpower website on "Employer's Guide: Migrant Domestic Worker" under "Rest Days, Health and Well-Being."

91 **The only exception is Canada:** Anju Mary Paul, "Stepwise International Migration: A Multistage Migration Pattern for the Aspiring Migrant," *American Journal of Sociology* 116, no. 6 (2011): 1842–86.
92 **"fly now, pay later":** Parreñas, *Servants of Globalization*, 13.
93 **government levy of S$300:** This levy rate is for families without children or other dependents. The monthly levy for those with dependents is much less, at S$60.
93 **Historian Filomeno Aguilar Jr.:** Filomeno Aguilar Jr., *Migration Revolution: Philippine Nationhood and Class Relations in a Globalized Age* (National University of Singapore, 2014), 11.
96 **"pernicious ignorance":** Dotson, "Tracking Epistemic Violence," 238.
99 **Palestinian literary critic:** Said, *Orientalism*.
103 **"fictitious commodity":** Karl Polanyi, *The Great Transformation* (1944; Beacon Press, 2001), 72–80.
104 **notion of "positive liberty":** Christman, "Liberalism and Individual Positive Freedom."
104 **agnotology:** Robert Proctor, "Agnotology: A Missing Term to Describe the Cultural Production of Ignorance," in *Agnotology: The Making and Unmaking of Ignorance*, ed. Robert Proctor and Londa Schiebinger (Stanford University Press, 2008), 8–20.

CONCLUSION: HOW TO FIGHT FORCED LABOR

115 **implemented a mandatory day off:** These countries implemented a day off soon after the adoption of this convention: Kingdom of Saudi Arabia in 2012, Singapore in 2013, and United Arab Emirates in 2014.
116 **dizzying number of reports:** These Human Rights Watch reports are *For a Better Life: Migrant Worker Abuse in Bahrain and the Government Reform Agenda*; *"I Already Bought You": Abuse and Exploitation of Female Migrant Domestic Workers in the United Arab Emirates*; *"I Was Sold": Abuse and Exploitation of Migrant Domestic Workers in Oman*; *"Working Like a Robot": Abuse of Tanzanian Domestic Workers in Oman and the United Arab Emirates*; and *Lebanon: Abolish Kafala (Sponsorship) System*.
117 **moral accountability:** Adelle Blackett, *Everyday Transgressions: Domestic Workers' Transnational Challenge to International Labor Law* (Cornell University Press, 2019); Jennifer Fish, *Domestic Workers of the World Unite! A Global Movement for Dignity and Human Rights* (New York University Press, 2017).

117 **Fair Labor Standards Act of 1938:** Evelyn Nakano Glenn, *Forced to Care: Coercion and Caregiving in America* (Harvard University Press, 2010), 137–47.

119 **randomized experiment:** Toman Barsbai et al., "Picture This: Social Distance and the Mistreatment of Migrant Workers," Working Papers in Economics and Statistics 2022-17, University of Innsbruck, 2022.

INDEX

Page numbers after 127 refer to notes.

A-3 visas, 38
abortion, 62, 136
"absconding," 64
Abu Dhabi, 66
Abu Sayyaf terrorist group, 56
abuse, 4–5, 38–43, 63–69
   criminalizing abuse, 117, 137
   cultural factors of, 35
   diminished autonomy, 57–59
   domestic abuse, 47
   emotional coercion/entrapment, 43, 45–46, 48
   family abuse and kin-based servitude, 29
   hotlines, 36–37, 39, 41
   how indenture engenders, 14–15
   lack of recourse, 11
   love as an enabler of, 47
   racist self-deflection among abusive Western expats, 96–97, 100–102
   rape, 51–54, 56
   the prospects of escape, 58
   sexual exploitation, 6, 9, 10, 12–13, 62, 125
   "structural violence," 66
   when employers admit, 16
"adoption" of poorer children, 18

agnotology (the study of ignorance), 104. *See also* pernicious ignorance
Aguilar, Filomeno, Jr., 93
Al Qaeda, 56
alipin namamahay ("slave who is housed"), 25
alipin sagigilid ("slave in the corners"), 25
American dream, 21, 41
American Institute of Foreign Study, 13
amnesty, in the United States, 39, 44
anti-exploiter, being an, 76, 77–79, 95, 109, 112, 119–21
anti-trafficking as a policy orientation, 7–8, 109, 113–15
Asuncion, Leticia, 21–22, 24–25, 28–35, 39, 42, 48–49
Atlantic, The (magazine), 18, 21–50, 111–12
au pairs, 13–15, 39, 65–66, 111, 131

B-1 visas, 39
Bahrain, 53, 116
Bales, Kevin, 5–6, 8–10, 38, 125
Ballard, Tim, 7–8
Banerjee, Pallavi, 75

INDEX

Bangladesh, 136
Bangsamoro Autonomous Region, Philippines, 55–56, 58
Barsbai, Toman, 118
Bearden, Sandra Luz, 41
Bhatt, Amy, 75
Blackett, Adelle, 117
Blinken, Antony, 5
bodily autonomy, 51–52
    diminished autonomy and abuse of workers, 57–59
    corporal management of domestic workers, 73–74
    the embodied existence of the worker, 78
    preventing cohabitation with family, 62
    See also indenture; time
Bourgois, Philippe, 11
Brazil, 4, 13–14, 18, 26, 34
Brennan, Denise, 11, 40
bureaucracy, 102, 104
Burmese fishermen in Thailand, 20

Cadena brothers of Mexico, 4, 8
Calhoun, John C., 18
California, 14, 41, 113, 116
Calimlim, Jefferson and Elnora, 41, 42
Cameroon, 34
Canada, 54, 64–65, 91–92, 115, 118, 135
capitalism, 20, 95–96
    destitution/extreme poverty, 4, 19–20, 43–44
    the "fictitious commodities" of, 103
    maid agencies flooding the labor market, 101
    "market price," 103–4
    the rational, price-sensitive decisions that lead to being trafficked, 55
    subjugation through labor market dynamics, 100–109
care workers, live-in vs. live-out, 117
chattel slavery, 5, 21, 24–25
children, 1–4
    "adoption" of poorer children, 18
    child domestic workers in Ghana, 4, 18, 34
    domestic work in childcare, 23, 28–29, 35–36, 57, 83–84
    of employers, 3–4, 97
    familial work arrangements in the Philippines, 30–36
    "raised daughters" of Brazil, 4, 26
    restavek in Haiti, 4, 26
    of trafficked workers, 56
    treating domestic workers like, 19, 104, 107
Christman, John, 76
Coalition for Humane Immigrant Rights of Los Angeles, 113
co-ethnic exploitation, 41–42
Cole, Teju, 16
Colombia, 13, 20, 27
compulsory labor. *See* forced labor
Connecticut, 116
Constable, Nicole, 74, 87
consulates. *See* diplomatic and consular affairs
contracts
    "contract slavery," 5, 38
    "contract substitution," 62
    cost of breaking, for employees, 63–64, 94, 137

cost of breaking, for employers, 61
cost of securing, for labor migration, 135
employer contracts, 120
for foreign nurses, 75, 138
importance of, 120
a look at contract negotiations at one agency, 79–93
rational decision making in, 55, 104, 107
See also indenture
Convention 189 (Convention Concerning Decent Work for Domestic Workers), 90, 114–15, 117
Cox, Benedicta, 40–43, 46–47
crime
criminalization of trafficking, 113–14
criminalization of undocumented workers, 39–40, 64
forced labor as a crime, 40, 96, 110–14
organized crime syndicates, 4, 7–8, 10
prostitution, 3, 4, 7, 9–10, 125
See also abuse; human trafficking
Criminal Investigation Department (Dubai), 57
Cuban migrants in Miami, 41–42
culture, 7, 17–19
co-ethnic exploitation through, 41–42
cultural factors of abuse, 35
explaining employers' behaviors, 96, 99–100
Filipino culture and forced labor arrangements, 24–29, 31–35
when local norms violate human rights, 121
See also Filipino diaspora; Western culture
Curaçao, 27

Damayan Migrant Workers in New York City, 113
days off
buyouts of, 90
as a form of corporal management, 73–76
denial of, 36–37, 44, 62, 69, 84, 94, 96–99, 104, 106, 113, 116
laws guaranteeing, 90, 115, 140
mandatory days off in Singapore, 90, 94, 115, 140
the traditional Sunday off, 70, 82
See also time
debt bondage, 5, 11–13, 15, 19, 66–70, 125
costs of migration, 54, 82–83, 135
culturally specific cases of, 25–26, 29, 32–34
how employers and maid agencies enable, 87–88, 91–95, 101–13
indebtedness and subjugation, 93–96
salary-deduction systems, 67, 109
in Singapore, 66–74, 90–96, 100–109, 111–13, 121, 135
"transfer maid" penalties, 68, 91
when unable to explain enslavement, 25–26
See also maid agencies
deflection, 18–19, 22, 54, 97, 99–100, 100–111
dehumanization, 112–13

democratic countries, 65, 112
Denmark, 54, 65, 115
destitution/extreme poverty, 4, 19–20, 43–44
diminished autonomy, 57–59
diplomatic and consular affairs
    consulates/embassies, 64, 66, 104
    passports and travel documents, 9, 90–91, 106–8
    residence visas, 61, 136
    tourist visas, 38, 54, 58–59, 61, 83, 136
    See also governance; immigration
Djibouti, 1
Doezema, Jo, 8
Domestic Worker Bill of Rights, 116–17
domestic workers
    attractiveness in hiring decisions, 87–88
    call for formal recognition of the occupation, 113–14
    corporal management of, 73–74
    double trap of indenture and debt, 68
    how employers exercise their authority over, 11–12, 15, 111–12
    infantilization of, 19, 104, 107
    live-in vs. live-out work, 14, 16, 37, 64–66, 117, 136, 137
    research on domestic workers globally, 15–20, 36, 43–46, 51–55, 66–67
    stories from the Filippino diaspora, 55–58, 67–74
    their possessions, 73
    transgender, 69–71
    See also contracts; migrant workers; working conditions
Donato, Katharine, 7
Dotson, Kristie, 96
Douglass, Frederick, 42
Dreby, Joanna, 35
Dubai, 15–17, 55–63, 66, 95–100, 112–15
    Americans living in, 59–60, 65, 136
    Criminal Investigation Department, 57
    the experience of a Sri Lankan migrant in, 58–62, 76, 77, 96–98, 100, 136
    food requirements for workers, 61
    living as a migrant domestic worker in, 55–64
    residence visas in, 61, 136
    "unauthorized" workers in, 57
    Western employers in, 15–17, 78–79, 96–100, 136
dubizzle.com, 59, 61

Elizabeth II of England, 1
embassies. *See* diplomatic and consular affairs
emotional coercion/entrapment, 43, 45–46, 48
employees. *See* domestic workers; migrant workers
"employer savior complex," 4, 11, 16–18, 94, 100–102, 108–9, 111–12, 119
employers, 4, 11–12, 16–20, 77–79
    attractiveness in hiring decisions, 87–88
    as complicit in forced labor, 95–96, 102, 105, 109

INDEX

contracts for, 120
deflection, 18–19, 22, 54, 97, 99–100, 100–111
effects of social distance upon, 118–19
exploitative expats from "the West," 63, 79–93, 96–100
feelings of entitlement, 63, 77–78
how to be an anti-exploiter, 76, 77–79, 95, 109, 112, 119–21
mandatory expenses paid by employers, 61
micromanagement by, 69, 73, 89
networks and organizations, 113, 117, 120
in the normalization of slave-like conditions., 69–72
the pernicious ignorance of, 19, 24, 96–97, 104, 112, 119, 121
punishment of, 113–14
their authority over domestic workers, 11–12, 15, 111–12
a visit to a maid agency, 79–93
See also contracts; wages; working conditions
Employers' Orientation Programme, 85, 139
Employment Agencies Act of 1958 (Singapore), 85
employment agencies. *See* maid agencies
England, 13, 65
British expats in Dubai, 16–17, 78, 98–99, 139
the story of Mohamed Farah, 1–4, 12, 42
English language proficiency, 81, 93

enslaver's logic, the, 8, 27
entitlement, feelings of, 63, 77–78
Ethiopia, 53, 115
expatriates, 63, 79–93, 96–100
Amanda, an American transplant in Singapore, 105–9
Beatrice, an Asian American in Singapore, 79–95, 112, 121, 139
Irene, an American in Dubai, 58–63, 76, 77–78, 96–100, 136
Matt, a British finance manager in Dubai, 98–100
Melinda, a small business owner in Singapore, 102–3
See also Western culture
exploitation
co-ethnic exploitation, 41–42
"exploiters" vs. "anti-exploiters," 77–109
the fight against, 110–21
organ removal, 7, 13, 125
sexual abuse, 7, 62
wage theft, 15, 18, 28, 52

Fair Labor Standards Act of 1938 (U.S.), 117
family- and kin-based enslavement, 2, 17, 18–19, 21–50
Farah, Mohamed, 1–4, 12, 42
FBI (Federal Bureau of Investigation), 40–41, 42, 46–47
female domesticity, ideology of, 19, 33, 35–36. *See also* women's lives
"fictitious commodities," 103
filhas de criação ("raised daughters") of Brazil, 4, 26

Filipino diaspora
  a case of enslavement among the, 18, 21–50, 111–12
  class tensions in the, 93
  common Tagalog expressions among the, 31, 40, 51–52
  forced labor among the, 37–41
  reputation of Filipino employers, 93–94
  returnees, 32, 95
  on social media, 65
  stories from domestic workers in the, 55–58, 67–74
  the view from two Filipino Americans, 18, 93
  at work, 9, 81–83
  See also Philippines
Fish, Jennifer, 117
"fixers," 56–57
food deprivation, 22, 25–26, 60–62, 70–71, 85–89, 92–93, 105
forced labor, 5–6, 10, 12–13, 36, 62–63, 125
  as a crime, 40, 96, 110–14
  exploiters of, 77–109
  fighting, 110–21
  forms of subjugation, 110–11
  how small favors add up, 120
  through indenture, 5, 11–15, 38–39, 58, 63–65, 68, 74–76, 78–79, 111, 121
  mobility in defining, 75–76
  teaching migrant workers about, 53
Forced Labour Convention of 1930, 125
Foreign Maid Scheme of 1978 (Singapore), 85
Forrest, Andrew, 6
France, 13
Free the Slaves, 5
freedom, 5
  the appearance of contentment, 42–43
  employers' micromanagement and infantilization, 19, 62, 104, 112
  "indentured mobility," 76, 138
  of an individual to choose unfreedom ("positive liberty"), 76, 104
  love as mechanism of enslavement, 46
  the maid agencies' role in restricting the freedom of workers, 90–91
  manumission, 23–25, 27–29, 44–46
Fujairah, 57

G-5 visas, 39
Gabaccia, Donna, 7
Gallagher, Anne, 6
Galtung, Johan, 66
Gardner, Andrew, 53
Germany, 13–14, 20
Ghana, 4, 18, 34
gift-giving as humanizing gesture, 119
Global Slavery Index, 6
governance
  bilateral agreements regarding minimum wages, 115–17, 136
  forced labor as a crime, 40, 96, 110–14
  national anti-trafficking laws, 113–14
  the need for international labor standards, 114–17
  poor enforcement, 111, 118

reforms to migrant labor practices, 65, 116, 136–38
whether domestic workers are included in general labor laws, 118
See also contracts; diplomatic and consular affairs; International Labour Organization (ILO)
Great Britain. *See* England
Gulf Cooperation Council countries, 37, 64, 98, 115
Gupta, Ashish, 14

H-1B visas, 75–76, 138
H-2B visas, 75, 137–38
Haiti, 4, 18, 26, 34
Hall, Shyima, 41
Hammond, James Henry, 18
Hand in Hand employer network, 113, 120
Hawaii, 116
home, 4, 14, 119–21
　as intimate space of confinement, 23–24, 37, 40–41, 73–74, 80–81, 105–7, 114
Hong Kong, 54, 66, 74, 87, 92, 119, 135
hotlines, 36–37, 39, 41
houselessness, 17
Human Rights Watch, 66, 113, 116, 140
human trafficking, 1–20, 125
　conditions enabling, 12–15
　glossary of terms related to, 125–26
　labor trafficking vs. sex trafficking, 4, 7–8, 12–13, 16, 114
　in the media, 4–5, 7–8
　the problem of numbers, 5–12
　See also exploitation; slavery; subjugation

Ibrahim, Abdel Nassar Eid Youssef, 41
ignorance. *See* pernicious ignorance
Ilagan, Marilou, 43–45
Illicit Flirtations (Parreñas), 138
Illinois, 14, 116
immigration
　costs of migration, 54, 82–83, 135
　legal permanent residency, 39, 64, 76, 134, 138
　the risks migrants take, 51–76
　"undocumented" or "unauthorized" workers, 11, 35, 37, 39–40, 57, 64
　visa runs, 83
　visa sponsorship, 10, 14–15, 37–39, 54, 63–66, 75, 82, 93, 134, 136, 137, 138
　See also governance; structural conditions; United States immigration
Immigration Reform and Control Act of 1986 (U.S.), 39
indebtedness. *See* debt bondage
indenture, 5, 11–15, 38–39, 58, 63–65, 68, 74–76, 78–79, 111, 121
"indentured mobility," 76, 138
Indonesia, 113, 115
　agencies in, 79–80, 82
　migrant workers from, 41, 52–53, 81–82
infantilization, 19, 104, 107
international affairs. *See* diplomatic and consular affairs; governance

INDEX

International Agreement for the Suppression of the "White Slave Traffic," 3
International Labour Organization (ILO), 6, 12, 36, 114–17, 131
  Convention 189 (Convention Concerning Decent Work for Domestic Workers), 90, 114–15, 117
  definition of "contract substitution," 62
  definition of "forced labor," 125
  Forced Labour Convention of 1930, 125
Israel, 13, 54, 65, 115
Italy, 64

J-1 Exchange Visitor Program, 13
Jamaica, 27
Japan, 10–12
Johor Bahru, Malaysia, 83

kafala system, 63–68, 75, 78, 100, 136–37
Kahin, Hussein Abdi (Mohamed Farah), 1–4, 12, 42
Khaleeji (Arabs of the UAE), 97–98
Kuwait, 37, 54, 56, 57, 64, 97, 100

labor
  agency manipulation of labor markets, 101
  labor market dynamics and subjugation, 100–109
  labor trafficking vs. sex trafficking, 4, 7–8, 12–13, 16, 114
  labor unions/organized labor, 64, 116
  limited labor rights and market participation, 117–18
  state labor laws, 14
  See also forced labor; wages; working conditions
Lammasniemi, Laura, 8
League of Nations Slavery Convention of 1926, 5, 126
Lebanon, 116
legal permanent residency, 39, 64, 76, 134, 138
Live-In Caregiver Program (Canada), 64–65
live-in vs. live-out work, 14, 16, 37, 64–66, 117, 136, 137
love, 23–24, 27, 29–30, 46–48, 49, 56
Lugasan, Fedelina, 40–41, 43, 46–47

maid agencies
  agency fees, 19, 61, 63, 66, 81, 101
  flooding the labor market, 101
  how employers and maid agencies enable debt bondage, 87–88, 91–95, 101–13
  a look at contract negotiations at one agency, 79–93
  saturated market of, 102
  in sending countries like Indonesia, 79–80, 82
  See also debt bondage
maids. *See* domestic workers
Malaysia, 13, 83, 91, 115, 129
mandatory rest. *See* days off
manumission (freedom from slavery), 23–25, 27–29, 44–46
"market price," 103–4
Martinez, Irma, 41
masakit (deep-seated sorrow), 31

INDEX

masculinity, specifically white male heroism, 7–8
Massachusetts, 116, 131
medical professions
   foreign-trained medical professionals, 39
   live-in vs. live-out care workers, 117
   nurses, 75, 138
Mexico, 13, 17, 37, 41
   Cadena brothers of Mexico, 4, 8
   "middlewomen" of, 35–36
migrant workers
   foreign nurses, 75, 138
   migrant mothers, 36
   migrant returnees who fare poorly, 53
   remittances, 30–31, 36, 45, 73
   the risks faced by, 51–76
   runaways, 64, 66
   software developers and engineers, 75
   working conditions, 64–76
   See also domestic workers
Migrant-Rights.org, 113, 116
migration. *See* immigration
Ministry of Manpower (Singapore), 79–80, 94, 139
mobility
   employer control over passports and travel documents, 9, 90–91, 106–8
   "indentured mobility," 76, 138
   limited labor rights and market participation, 117–18
   "two-week rule," 66
   See also indenture; slavery; subjugation
modern-day slavery, 5–6, 8, 11–12, 21, 23, 36, 41, 116, 125. *See also* forced labor; slavery; subjugation
Moro Muslim rebels, 55–56
Motelib, Amal Ahmed Ewis-abd, 41
Myanmar, 58, 80–81

"Nana Ebia." *See* Pulido-Gabertan, Lolita "Ebia"
natal alienation, 23, 31, 49, 110
National Domestic Workers Alliance, 15, 28, 45, 113, 116
National Human Trafficking Hotline, 36
Netherlands, 2, 65, 115
Nevada, 116
New Mexico, 116
New York City, 113
New York state, 14, 116
nongovernmental organizations, 113, 116
Norway, 65
nurses under contract, 75, 138

Office to Monitor and Combat Trafficking in Persons (U.S.), 9
Olympic Games, 1
Oman, 64, 116
Oregon, 14, 116
organ removal, 7, 13, 125
Orientalism, 18, 99–100
Overseas Workers Welfare Administration (Philippines), 52

Parreñas, Rhacel Salazar
   employers among her own family, 17, 37–38
   her own experience as an employer, 78*n*, 93–95

Parreñas, Rhacel Salazar (*continued*)
  Illicit Flirtations, 138
  notion of "indentured mobility," 76, 138
  on the problem of "zombie statistics," 6–9
  research methods of, 5–12, 55, 112
  research on domestic workers globally, 15–20, 36, 43–46, 51–55, 66–67
  visiting the family of a modern-day slave, 29–33, 49–50
  work among Filipino entertainers in Japan, 9–10
passports and travel documents, 9, 90–91, 106–8
Patterson, Orlando, 23, 27, 29, 31
peonage. *See* debt bondage
People (magazine), 46
permanent residency, 39, 64, 76, 134, 138
pernicious ignorance, 19, 24, 96–97, 104, 112, 119, 121
Philippines
  Abu Sayyaf terrorist group, 56
  Basilan, Bangsamoro Autonomous Region, 55–56, 58
  "fixers," 56–57
  mandatory predeparture seminars in the, 51–54, 58, 80, 115, 119
  the middle class of the, 139
  Moro Muslim rebels, 55–56
  two types of "slaves" in the, 25
  See also Filipino diaspora
Pilipino Workers Center of Southern California, 45, 113
Polanyi, Karl, 103
Polaris Project, 15, 36

Portes, Alejandro, 42
"positive liberty," 76, 104
possession of domestic workers by employers. *See* abuse; subjugation
possessions, owned by domestic workers, 73
pregnancy outside of marriage, 62
Prevention of Human Trafficking Act of 2014 (Singapore), 94, 114
Proctor, Robert, 104
prostitution, 3, 4, 7, 9–10, 125
Pulido, Eudocia Tomas (Lola Cosiang), 21–50
  an American slave, 36–42
  defenders of her enslavement, 42–43
  as a family member, 24–36
  her death and return home, 48–50
  role of love in her subjugation, 43–48
Pulido-Gabertan, Lolita "Ebia" (Nana Ebia), 31–33, 44–45, 48–50

Qatar, 37, 53, 58, 75, 136–37

race and racism
  campaigns against "white slavery," 3, 8
  co-ethnic exploitation, 41–42
  Orientalism, 18, 99–100
  racist self-deflection, 97, 99–100
  white male heroism, 7–8
  "white-savior industrial complex," 16
Rafael, Vicente, 24–27
"raised daughters" of Brazil, 4, 26
rape, 51–54, 56
Real Mo Farah, The (documentary), 1

INDEX

remittances, 30–31, 36, 45, 73
residence visas in Dubai, 61, 136
restavek in Haiti, 4, 26
Romero, Mary, 27
runaways, 64, 66

Said, Edward, 99
salary-deduction system, 67, 109
Saluja, Harit "Potee," 17
Saudi Arabia
    employers in, 14, 37, 119
    kafala system in, 64, 137, 138, 140
    regulations on domestic work, 14, 115
    reputation of, 36, 98
    skilled migrant engineers, 75
    workers in, 56–57
savior complexes, 16. *See also* "employer savior complex"
servitude, 1, 13, 25, 29, 32–34, 41, 125, 126
sexual exploitation, 6, 9, 10, 12–13, 62, 125
Singapore, 13, 15, 18–19, 54–55
    debt bondage in, 66–74, 90–96, 100–109, 111–13, 121, 135
    Employers' Orientation Programme, 85, 139
    Employment Agencies Act of 1958, 85
    feelings of entitlement, 78n
    Foreign Maid Scheme of 1978, 85
    as lacking minimum wage regulations, 19
    live-in employment only for domestic work, 65–66
    living as a migrant domestic worker in, 79–93

    mandatory days off in, 90, 94, 115, 140
    the middle class in, 139
    Ministry of Manpower, 79–80, 94, 139
    monthly levy rate on hiring domestic workers, 93, 140
    practice of withholding wages, 10–11, 19, 66–68, 86–87, 94–95
    Prevention of Human Trafficking Act of 2014, 94, 114
Slavery Convention of 1926, 5, 126
slavery, 5–6, 8, 11–12, 21–50, 23, 36, 41, 116, 125
    the appearance of contentment among the enslaved, 42–43, 46
    chattel slavery, 5, 21, 24–25
    "contract slavery," 5, 38
    culturally specific cases of, 25–26, 29, 32–34
    the enslaver's logic, 8, 27
    freedom from slavery (manumission), 23–25, 27–29, 44–46
    the power of love to enslave, 23–24, 27, 29–30, 46–48, 49, 56
    "slave in the house" vs. "slave next door," 25
    Spain under Muslim rule, 27–29
    "white slavery," 3, 8
Social Security contributions, 45, 93
software developers, visas for, 75
Somali civil war, 1
Sound of Freedom (film), 7–8
South Africa, 27
Spain under Muslim rule, 27–29
sponsorship, 10, 14–15, 37–39, 54, 63–66, 75, 82, 93, 134, 136, 137, 138

Sri Lanka, 53, 58
state labor laws, 14
state minimum wage, 14, 131
statistics, 5–9, 36
structural conditions, 111–12
    employers and racialist structures of subjugation, 96–100
    social constraints on choice, 76
    social structures of race and nationality, 95–96, 109
    See also capitalism; culture; governance; immigration
"structural violence," 66
"structural vulnerability," 11–13, 20
subjugation, 4, 7–11, 22, 110–11, 120
    through bureaucracy, 102, 104
    emotional coercion/entrapment, 43, 45–46, 48
    employers and racialist structures of, 96–100
    family- and kin-based enslavement, 2, 17, 18–19, 21–50
    food deprivation, 22, 25–26, 60–62, 70–71, 85–89, 92–93, 105
    indebtedness and, 93–96
    indenture, 5, 11–15, 38–39, 58, 63–65, 68, 74–76, 78–79, 111, 121
    labor market dynamics and, 100–109
    servitude, 1, 13, 25, 29, 32–34, 41, 125, 126
    social pressures and, 107–9, 112
    through visa sponsorship, 10, 14–15, 37–39, 54, 63–66, 75, 82, 93, 134, 136, 137, 138
    of women, through their love, 23–24, 27, 29–30, 46–48, 49, 56
    See also debt bondage (peonage); forced labor; indenture; slavery
Sun, The (newspaper), 3
Sundays off, 70, 82
Supplemental Security Income (SSI), 44
Switzerland, 80–81

Taiwan, 92, 115, 135
Taken (film), 4–5, 7, 41, 70
Thailand, 20, 58
time
    agency fees calculated by time, 91
    employers' perceived ownership of, 68–69, 77–78, 88–89, 96–97, 112–13
    free time for employees, 15, 72–73
    how the intimate space of the home exacerbates, 120
    task-based work conditions, 76, 77–79
    See also days off
Tizon, Alex, 18, 21–50, 111–12
Tizon, Melissa, 46
tourist visas, 38, 54, 58–59, 61, 83, 136
traffickers, 1–4
    Cadena brothers of Mexico, 4, 8
    "fixers" in the Philippines, 56–57
    yakuza, 10
    See also employers; human trafficking; maid agencies
Trafficking in Persons Report, 5–6, 8, 9–10
Trafficking Victims Protection Act of 2000 (U.S.), 114
trafficking. *See* human trafficking
"transfer maid" penalties, 68, 91
transgender domestic workers, 69–71

Transient Workers Count Too (Singapore), 116
Triandafyllidou, Anna, 58
Turkey, 13, 65–66

"undocumented" or "unauthorized" workers, 11, 35, 37, 39–40, 57, 64
United Arab Emirates
 abortion access in, 62, 136
 "absconding," 64
 Abu Dhabi, 66
 Fujairah, 57
 kafala system, 63–68, 75, 78, 100, 136–37
 as lacking minimum wage regulations, 60
 laws criminalizing trafficking, 114
 pregnancy outside of marriage, 62
 See also Dubai
United Kingdom. *See* England
United Nations, 3, 12–13, 110, 113
 Convention Against Transnational Organized Crime, 125
 High Commissioner for Human Rights, 6
 Office on Drugs and Crime, 8
 Protocol to Prevent, Suppress, and Punish Trafficking in Persons (2000), 114, 125
United States
 amnesty in the, 39, 44
 au pairs in the, 13–15, 39, 65–66, 111, 131
 Cuban migrants in Miami, 41–42
 FBI (Federal Bureau of Investigation), 40–41, 42, 46–47
 ignoring its own trafficking until 2010, 9

Office to Monitor and Combat Trafficking in Persons (U.S.), 9
 a modern-day American slave, 21–50
 Social Security contributions, 45, 93
 state labor laws, 14
 state minimum wage, 14, 131
 Supplemental Security Income (SSI), 44
United States immigration
 the "American dream," 21, 41
 A-3 visas, 38
 B-1 visas, 39
 exclusionary immigration policies, 11, 38–39
 G-5 visas, 39
 H-1B visas, 75–76, 138
 H-2B visas, 75, 137–38
 J-1 Exchange Visitor Program, 13
 permanent residency, 39, 64, 76, 134, 138
 visa lottery, 75
U.S. Au Pair Inc., 14
U.S. Congress, 9
 Fair Labor Standards Act of 1938 (U.S.), 117
 Immigration Reform and Control Act of 1986, 39
 Trafficking Victims Protection Act of 2000, 114
 Victims of Trafficking and Violence Protection Act, 9
U.S. Court of Appeals for the First Circuit, 131
U.S. Department of Labor, 14
U.S. Department of State, 5–6, 8, 9–10, 14

U.S. Government Accountability
    Office, 10
U.S. Information Agency (American
    Institute of Foreign Study), 13

Vance, Carole, 7
Venezuela, 20
Victims of Trafficking and Violence
    Protection Act (U.S.), 9
violence. *See* abuse; crime
Virginia, 116
Vlieger, Antoinette, 53

wages
   agency manipulation of labor
       markets, 101
   bilateral agreements regarding minimum wages, 115–17, 136
   countries that lack minimum
       wages, 19, 60
   docking wages for employer
       expenses and agency fees, 14–15,
       57, 59
   an employer's view of "fair wages,"
       98
   inability to retire, 45
   minimum wage in the United
       States, 14, 17, 36–38, 40, 117,
       121, 131
   mobility as rationalization for low
       wages, 16–17
   overtime pay, 36, 65, 117
   pay grades by nationality, 81
   paying "below-market wages,"
       112–13
   paying less than minimum wages,
       37–38
   "transfer maid" penalties, 68, 91

wage theft, 15, 18, 28, 52
withholding wages in Singapore,
    10–11, 19, 66–68, 86–87, 94–95
Walk Free, 6
Washington, DC, 14
Watkinson, Alan, 2
Weitzer, Ronald, 8–9
Western culture
   exploitative domestic-labor
       arrangements in, 13–15
   exploitative expats abroad, 63,
       79–93, 96–100
   Orientalism and the "employer
       savior complex," 18, 99–100
   See also employers
white male heroism, 7–8
"white slavery," 3, 8
"white-savior industrial complex," 16
women's lives
   as domestic workers, 12, 19, 51–52,
       54–55
   ideology of female domesticity, 19,
       33, 35–36
   Mexico's "middlewomen," 35–36
   as migrant domestic workers in
       Singapore, 79–93
   as migrant domestic workers in the
       United Arab Emirates, 55–64
   pregnancy outside of marriage, 62
   prostitution, 3, 4, 7, 9–10, 125
   rape, 51–54, 56
   sexual exploitation, 6, 9, 10, 12–13,
       62, 125
women's rights
   abortion, 62, 136
   on the subjugation of women, 4,
       7–11, 22, 110–11, 120
   See also bodily autonomy; freedom

working conditions, 64–76
   Domestic Worker Bill of Rights, 116–17
   moral standards and, 121
   the need for international standards, 114–17
   pernicious ignorance regarding, 19, 37, 40, 84, 89–90, 100
   in Singapore, 69–74
   task-based work conditions, 76, 77–79
   See also abuse; time; wages
World Cup 2022 (Qatar), 58, 75

yakuza, 10

Zhang, Sheldon, 7
"zombie statistics," 6–9

Norton Shorts

BRILLIANCE WITH BREVITY

W. W. Norton & Company has been independent since 1923, when William Warder Norton and Mary (Polly) D. Herter Norton first published lectures delivered at the People's Institute, the adult education division of New York City's Cooper Union. In the 1950s, Polly Norton transferred control of the company to its employees.

One hundred years after its founding, W. W. Norton & Company inaugurates a new century of visionary independent publishing with Norton Shorts. Written by leading-edge scholars, these eye-opening books deliver bold thinking and fresh perspectives in under two hundred pages.

Available Fall 2025

Imagination: A Manifesto by Ruha Benjamin

What's Real About Race?: Untangling Science, Genetics, and Society by Rina Bliss

Offshore: Stealth Wealth and the New Colonialism by Brooke Harrington

Sex Beyond "Yes": Pleasure and Agency for Everyone by Quill R Kukla

Fewer Rules, Better People: The Case for Discretion by Barry Lam

Explorers: A New History by Matthew Lockwood

Wild Girls: How the Outdoors Shaped the Women Who Challenged a Nation by Tiya Miles

The Trafficker Next Door: How Household Employers Exploit Domestic Workers by Rhacel Salazar Parreñas

The Moral Circle: Who Matters, What Matters, and Why by Jeff Sebo

Against Technoableism: Rethinking Who Needs Improvement by Ashley Shew

Fear Less: Poetry in Perilous Times by Tracy K. Smith

Literary Theory for Robots: How Computers Learned to Write by Dennis Yi Tenen

Forthcoming

Mehrsa Baradaran on the racial wealth gap

Merlin Chowkwanyun on the social determinants of health

Daniel Aldana Cohen on eco-apartheid

Jim Downs on cultural healing

Reginald K. Ellis on Black education versus Black freedom

Nicole Eustace on settler colonialism

Agustín Fuentes on human nature

Justene Hill Edwards on the history of inequality in America

Destin Jenkins on a short history of debt

Kelly Lytle Hernández on the immigration regime in America

Natalia Molina on the myth of assimilation

Tony Perry on water in African American culture and history

Beth Piatote on living with history

Ashanté Reese on the transformative possibilities of food

Daniel Steinmetz-Jenkins on religion and populism

Onaje X. O. Woodbine on transcendence in sports